THE SCRIPT OF
ELIZABETH

THE SCRIPT OF
ELIZABETH

MICHAEL HIRST

BOXTREE

First published 1998 by Boxtree
an imprint of Macmillan Publishers Ltd
25 Eccleston Place London SW1W 9NF
and Basingstoke

Associated companies throughout the world

ISBN 0 7522 2454 9

9 8 7 6 5 4 3 2 1

A CIP catalogue record for this book is available from
the British Library.

Designed by: Dan Newman
Photographs by Alex Bailey
Printed by: The Bath Press Group

CONTENTS

INTRODUCTION

BY MICHAEL HIRST

The first thing to say about *Elizabeth* is that it is a film, not a documentary. Many of the scenes are based on historical fact (or what passes for historical fact), but others are not. Of course, before I even began to write I had done a huge amount of historical research; but the reason behind the research was to discover a way into the material, a lever to shift it with, what film people call 'an angle'. Unlike life, films have to have a dramatic shape.

Elizabeth lived and reigned a long time and there were many episodes in her life which could have provided, at least, a good starting point. I decided pretty early on, however, that I wanted to show her as a young woman – the young woman arrested for treason and afraid for her life; the young woman passionately in love with Robert Dudley – and not the white-faced, pearl-encrusted icon of her later years, and of historical memory. Indeed, I was intrigued to know how and why that iconograph had been created; what where the motivations, political and personal, behind the myth of the Virgin Queen? What did Elizabeth, as a Queen, gain by its creation and what, if anything, did she lose as a woman? And so, ironically, from the moment of the film's conception I also had its ending: the moment at which Elizabeth became 'historical', an icon, a public image with its deliberate but subtle echoes of the Virgin Mary.

The screenplay took over three years to write. A script, of course, is only ever a working document; unlike a play, for example, it has no finished form and continues, in effect, to be rewritten even as the film is being edited. *Elizabeth* went through drafts and changes too numerous to mention, too agonising to recall. Some of the changes were voluntary, as ideas and solutions superseded each other; others, more painful, were the result of financial constraints or simple practicalities. No writer, in the privacy of his or her imagination should ever feel constrained from imagining *anything* on screen, however extraordinary, however expensive. As my first mentor, the director Nicholas Roeg, told me: 'This is a film; an elephant could walk in the door here.' The trouble was, at some points in the film there were too many elephants in the script. There was a huge firework party and masque at Kenilworth Castle; a siege and a battle, with thousands of dead, and French whores pissing from the battlements over the corpses. Alas, both the party, and the whores, had to

go … but they remain like ghostly presences inside the script, still to me part of it, rotting down into its texture with a thousand other wonderful images and thoughts.

From the start, one of my problems was to condense so much rich material into such a little space. I wanted the film to be intimate and personal … to vibrate with the nervous system of a young woman … but also to have a sense of scale, of grandeur, for the young woman was also a Queen. For me, the midsummer pageant on the Thames performed both these functions, and was always a pivotal and seminal scene. On this night, drunk with love, Elizabeth and Dudley, by then Earl of Leicester, teased the Spanish Ambassador and asked him to marry them, then and there. It is one of the great romantic images in European culture – part of the iconography of romantic love. T.S. Eliot used it in 'The Waste Land', comparing the lovers to Anthony and Cleopatra:

> *Elizabeth and Leicester*
> *Beating oars*
> *The stern was formed*
> *A gilded shell*
> *Red and gold …*

Such scenes have a resonance for me over and above their narrative importance … but since this is a film, they must also carry the narrative forward, serve a function. Hence, at this point, we decided to interrupt the idyll, to reintroduce political reality, in the shape of the assassination attempt. But to hold these two things in tension – the independent and free content of the scene, and then its narrative function – is, I think, one of the principal jobs of the screenwriter.

I also wanted the film to be thick with plots. When she first came to the throne, Elizabeth was in an extraordinarily vulnerable position; indeed, one of her courtiers gave her only a year to survive. Some of the

conspiracies that flourished around her, then and later, were complex, labyrinthine and bizarre. On the surface most of them were motivated by religion, but beneath that seethed a mass of other motives – to do with power, court politics, national interest and sex. By allowing into the script a number of plots, rather than teasing out the thread of one, I knew I risked leaving the door of confusion, if not open, then at least ajar. But the risk seemed worthwhile. More than a single threat, I wanted to expose Elizabeth to this climate of conspiracy, to the realities of Renaissance politics. In so doing, of course, I made myself, as a writer, the most Machievellian of all her courtiers!

Thirdly, I wanted to show the immediate conjunction between beauty and violence. For me, this was a key not only to the Elizabethan Age, but to the film. I was already steeped in Elizabethan poetry, particularly the work of Sir Thomas Wyatt, which showed this: the extreme uncertainty of life, particularly court life, and the sudden shift between rapture and terror, life and death. One of Wyatt's poems is, invisibly, behind the whole film:

> *They flee from me that sometime did me seek,*
> *With naked foot stalking in my chamber;*
> *I have seen them gentle, tame and meek,*
> *That now are wild, and do not remember*
> *That some time they put themselves in danger*
> *To take bread at my hand; and now they range*
> *Busily seeking with a continual change.*

Film is a brilliant medium for showing such violent juxtapositions. And it seemed to me that their vivid and dramatic use – like the burning of the martyrs and the dancing of the women – could as a matter of fact bring us much closer to some kind of historical 'truth' than any amount of dead facts and inert details … whether of

costume, language or furniture. The film itself, the way it was made, as much as its content, was the message.

Many of the changes in the earlier drafts were the result of trying to develop those three major strands of the story. But then came the greatest and most profound change of all: Shekhar Kapur walked in the door. The idea of an Indian directing a quintessentially English subject must have surprised some – but it delighted me. Shekhar had made a remarkable film called *Bandit Queen* (no relation), which was raw with emotion … not a quality easily associated with British films, at least 'historical' ones. He brought with him no preconceptions about Elizabeth. Without perhaps even being conscious of it, many English people are protective about the image – and virginity – of Elizabeth I; after all, she remains one of the greatest icons in our history. But the last thing the film needed was a reverential camera. Shekhar's greatest gift, actually, was that he never saw the film as being 'historical' at all; for him, it was always about people. He wanted more of a sense of Elizabeth as a woman, a human being. This was important. Most historical characters are approached from the outside: we take what we know about how they dressed, spoke, behaved, and try to recreate them from these externals. Shekhar needed to know about the character from the inside. Elizabeth was a great Queen – but her first reality was as a woman. This surprised even some of her contemporaries: 'Good God,' one man remarked as her carriage rolled past, 'the Queen is a woman!'

Shekhar took nothing for granted; he wanted it torn apart, examined, and only then, temporarily, put back together again. His principal line – the one I grew to dread – was 'I want more'. I dreaded it because, even if he liked a scene, or perhaps particularly if he liked it, he still 'wanted more'. More of what? More of everything: more emotion, or more tension, or more danger, or … well, just more. Eventually, he 'wanted more' from the actors, too, and the director of photography, the designer, the producer … even, I think, of his driver. Shekhar needs to push people to their limits. But he is not a dictator. For the first time in my career I was invited and encouraged on to the set, to give my opinions on the scenes and set-ups, to argue with and encourage the actors. I have the profoundest respect for Shekhar, who is still – unbelievably – one of my best friends. I admire his abilities – and nothing gave me greater pleasure, or a more visceral thrill, than watching the rushes and perceiving images that were often better than the ones I had carried so long in my head. For many screenwriters, the finished film is only a pale substitute for the film that has been running in the private screening rooms of their imaginations.

Finally, I would like to acknowledge the contribution to the screenplay made by Tim Bevan and Debra Hayward of Working Title. They hired me, they were with me when I read out scraps of poems, thoughts, ideas and scenes that I had scribbled on the back of a piece of wallpaper, and which finally coalesced into the idea for the film. And then, throughout its long gestation, they never lost faith. Film-making is a difficult business, but it is surprisingly full of good people.

But perhaps I should add a coda. For putting Elizabeth into bed with Dudley I have already been branded a heretic. Now neither you nor I, nor any of the rent-a-quote historians know with any certainty whether they were actually lovers. Nobody disputes that they behaved like lovers, but Elizabeth's virginity is still highly prized, and an essential part of her status as an icon. All I want to say is this: by showing them as lovers I have not changed the course of English history, nor proved that the historical Elizabeth slept with and enjoyed the historical Dudley. The characters in the film sleep with one another, because that is the logical expression of their desire, their passion, their love ... and because it puts into the sharpest relief Elizabeth's choices, the dangers she faced as a woman and as a Queen. It does not detract at all from her decision to be 'a virgin', to sacrifice her personal happiness, and her chance of having children, in favour of the greater happiness and security of her people. If anything, it is only a small nudge in the direction of romanticism ... 'to prove', as Philip Larkin said, 'our almost instincts almost true/what remains of us, is love'.

M.H.

The young Elizabeth (Cate Blanchett)

PUBLISHER'S NOTE: *What follows is the shooting script, correct at the time of going to press. The final film may differ in some respects.*

INT. ROOM, BISHOPSGATE, LONDON – DAY

We look down from above on A WOMAN's head. As we watch, her hair is roughly chopped off.

WOMAN MARTYR: I will praise the Lord, and so shall be saved from mine enemies. For the waves of death have closed about me, and the floods of Belial have feared me. The cords of Hell have compassed me about, and the snares of death have overtaken me.

These words appear on the screen: ENGLAND, 1554.
   The chopping goes on. We also see the helmets of the GUARDS in this bare room. Nearby, A MAN lies curled up on the floor.

MALE MARTYR: Pater, Filius, et Spiritus Sanctus.

His head is roughly shaved. The GUARD hacks away brutally at THE WOMAN's shorn head. It starts to bleed. He dips the knife in a bowl of water – it turns red. She whimpers, and tries to draw her head away, but he goes on hacking. Her fingers touch the chains of her shackles like beads on a rosary.

WOMAN MARTYR: I will praise the Lord, and so shall be saved from mine enemies. For the waves of death have closed about me, and the floods of Belial have feared me. The cords of Hell have compassed me about, and the snares of death have overtaken me.

Then, still seen from above, A YOUNG MAN's hair is chopped off. The two GUARDS hack away at his head.

EXT. BISHOPSGATE, LONDON – DAY

The three shaven MARTYRS are led out into the open. We hear a great WUMPH of noise, as if from a great crowd. See flaring torches. The PRIESTS follow. From above – the MARTYRS are bound to a stake. BISHOP GARDINER, cold and vicious, watches from a platform.

GARDINER: By order of their gracious Majesties, Queen Mary and King Philip II, we are come to witness the burning of these heretics, who have denied the authority of the one true Catholic Church, and of his Holiness the Pope. Let them burn for all eternity, in the flames of hell ...

He gives a signal and A MAN carrying a torch sets light to the piles of wood. As the wood begins to burn, the WOMAN struggles against her bonds with an increasing frenzy. A MONK holds a cross up to her.

WOMAN MARTYR: In my tribulation I called to the Lord, and cried to my God. And he heard my voice cry out in his temple, and my cry entered into his ears. And the earth trembled and quoke, and the foundations of heaven moved and shook, because he was angry. I will praise the Lord, and so shall be saved from mine enemies. For the waves of death have closed about me, and the floods of Belial have feared me. The cords of Hell have compassed me about, and the snares of death have overtaken me. *(repeats/chants)*

MALE MARTYR: Benedicat te Omnipotens Deus, Pater, Filius et Spiritus Sanctus. (repeats/chants)

The crowd cry out.

VOICE: God give you strength and patience, Master Ridley, not to recant! Bless you.

YOUTH: Burn them!

The fires burn slowly, the flames still licking at the MARTYRS' lower limbs. One of the MEN cries out.

MARTYR: For the love of God, friends, I burn too slowly!

There is a sudden hush.

OLDER WOMAN: Help them!

Then, in open defiance, and much to GARDINER's obvious disgust, people start to push their way through the cordon of SOLDIERS and heap more wood on the flames – which now crackle and leap, the MARTYRS' clothing all ablaze, their bodies like human torches.
   We move into wide shot as the huge CROWD is thrown and pushed back by armed SOLDIERS on horseback.

Opposite top: *A female martyr is shaved*

Opposite bottom: *The bishops watch as the martyrs are led out before the crowd*

Above and right: *The martyrs are tied up and burnt at the stake*

Mary Tudor (Kathy Burke) with her husband King Philip

DISSOLVE TO: EXT. WHITEHALL PALACE, LONDON – DAY

The bells are ringing – from every church tower in London.

We are in a long, roofed colonnade leading into the palace, which is crowded with COURTIERS. The DUKE OF NORFOLK, England's greatest noble, enters with his RETINUE in their yellow livery and his great hunting dogs, creating a STIR as they walk through into the Queen's Privy Chambers.

INT. QUEEN'S PRIVY CHAMBERS, WHITEHALL PALACE – DAY

NORFOLK enters a corridor leading to the Privy Chambers. He sweeps inside, as if he owns the place. He is magnificently dressed, a great picture of arrogance. He is setting the pace, and he is furious. The COURTIERS make way for him, bow with the deepest reverence. The palace CHAMBERLAIN falls in beside him, struggling to keep pace.

CHAMBERLAIN *(to NORFOLK)*: The Queen is with child!

The impact of this news on NORFOLK is not betrayed by him at all. He does not even glance at the CHAMBERLAIN.

NORFOLK: They should have consulted me before they rang the bells.

As he sweeps up the steps to the royal apartments, LETTICE appears out of the shadows. NORFOLK passes and acknowledges her presence. She follows him.

NORFOLK: It is true?

LETTICE *(low)*: There are symptoms. She has ceased to bleed, her breasts have produced some milk, and her stomach is swollen ...

Sotto voce, familiar – these two have a history.

NORFOLK: It is true?

LETTICE: The King has not shared her bed for many months. He has a repugnance for it ...
(A beat, pointed) As lately your Grace has for mine.

NORFOLK smiles, as he raises his hand and strokes her face and lips, turns away ...

CUT TO: INT. MARY'S BEDCHAMBER, WHITEHALL PALACE – DAY

NORFOLK strides inside. It is a large and very dark room filled with images of the Virgin and Child, icons and candles.

QUEEN MARY and her small, dapper Spanish husband, PHILIP II, sit on their thrones. A FEMALE DWARF is standing next to the QUEEN.

QUEEN MARY is small and, although only in her mid thirties, looks prematurely old, with few remaining teeth and her thin hair scraped back from her forehead. Her stomach is visibly swollen.

Out of the shadows appear the faces of a NUN and PRIESTS. Then the faces, like portraits, of her COUNCILLORS: BISHOP GARDINER, the EARLS OF SUSSEX and ARUNDEL ...

Near to the KING stands the haughty Spanish Ambassador, ALVARO DE LA QUADRA. NORFOLK approaches the KING and QUEEN, bows ornately.

NORFOLK: Your Majesties ... This is most wondrous news!

MARY's face is suffused with happiness and irradiated by a smile – and she looks lovingly upon the KING.

MARY: Indeed. We do thank God for this, our most happy condition.

She takes the KING's hand. The KING's face remains devoid of expression. NORFOLK looks at him.

NORFOLK: We must also thank his Majesty, for this blessed event ... which is nothing short of a miracle!

The KING remains impassive.

MARY: What news, my Lords, of the rebellion against our authority?

SUSSEX: Madam, it is safely dispatched – thanks to his Grace ...

He looks at NORFOLK.

NORFOLK: Sir Thomas Wyatt and the other leaders are already dealt with.

GARDINER: But if they had succeeded, these Protestants and heretics meant to place your sister upon the throne.

ARUNDEL: There is no proof against the Lady Elizabeth!

NORFOLK (*looks across to ARUNDEL*)**:** She is plainly guilty.

SUSSEX: What need is there of proof?

GARDINER: As long as she remains alive, there will be plots to raise her to the throne.

MARY nods and, after a moment, looks at ALVARO.

MARY: Ambassador?

ALVARO glances at the KING, whose face is still completely devoid of expression.

ALVARO: I agree with his Grace. She is a heretic. She must never be allowed to succeed.

ARUNDEL: But if she were brought properly to trial, she would be found not guilty – and we would all be condemned. She has many friends in Parliament …

MARY's face contorts with anger.

MARY: My sister was born of that whore Anne Boleyn. She was born a bastard. She will never rule England!

Everyone is silenced by her hysterical outburst. Then, equally abruptly, she is poised again and looks at NORFOLK.

MARY: Your Grace will find some proof of her treachery – I am most sure of it!

The Dance Tutor (Wayne Sleep)

CUT TO: EXT. APPROACH TO HATFIELD HOUSE, SURREY – DAY

A hollow TICK-TOCK sound. A white HORSE galloping across the fields. LORD ROBERT DUDLEY, saturnine good looks, expert horseman, heels dug into the horse's flanks. Behind him a pretty young girl, ISABEL, squeals in excitement and fear as he urges the horse on.

EXT. HATFIELD HOUSE, SURREY – DAY

We find the source of the tick-tock sound – a DANCE TUTOR hitting a hollow piece of wood with a stick, accompanying a group of YOUNG WOMEN dancing the galliard.
Close on a YOUNG WOMAN with red hair, ELIZABETH. The others are her LADIES-IN-WAITING. They are not taking the lesson very seriously, and keep falling out of step and giggling. ELIZABETH looks around.

DANCE TUTOR: Ladies, please. Control. Decorum.

ELIZABETH looks around. The DANCE TUTOR looks at her with obvious disapproval.

DANCE TUTOR: Madam, these steps are unseemly for a Lady! What would the gentlemen say?

ELIZABETH: The gentlemen, my lord, will not be looking at my feet!

The other LADIES giggle. DUDLEY pulls his horse to halt.
He lets ISABEL down to the ground and looks over.

DUDLEY: Who will be next, my ladies?

Some of the LADIES abandon the dance and run towards him, laughing and shrieking with delight. He looks past them and over at ELIZABETH, who continues to dance. The DANCE TUTOR beats time with the stick. He looks back at DUDLEY disapprovingly.
ELIZABETH is oblivious as he dismounts and walks towards her. The DANCE TUTOR backs away.

DUDLEY: May I join you, my Lady?

His eyes do not leave hers.

ELIZABETH: If it pleases you, Sir.

CUT TO: INT. HUNTING LODGE – EVENING

Music carries over to ELIZABETH and DUDLEY alone, dancing together, eyes locked. The dance is sensuous, not formal.

EXT. HATFIELD HOUSE, SURREY – DAY

KAT runs through the grounds. Panic-stricken, panting, glancing behind her. Cresting a rise, running down a steep grassy slope towards the hunting lodge ... Stumbling, falling in a heap, running on ...

INT. HUNTING LODGE – EVENING

ELIZABETH and DUDLEY dance on, oblivious.

INT. HUNTING LODGE – EVENING

DUDLEY and ELIZABETH in front of a fire. Sound of knock at the door.

ELIZABETH: They have come.

DUDLEY exits.

CUT TO: EXT. HUNTING LODGE – EVENING

KAT runs towards the lodge. She knocks on the door, and there is the sound of hooves. KAT turns to face them. A group of ARMED SOLDIERS, SUSSEX in the midst, ride toward the lodge.
   DUDLEY emerges. The HORSEMEN pull up in front of them and surround the house.

SUSSEX: Princess Elizabeth! Princess Elizabeth!

ELIZABETH joins DUDLEY.

SUSSEX *(cont'd)*: You are accused of conspiring with Sir Thomas Wyatt and others, against her Sovereign Majesty, and are arrested for treason. I am commanded to take you hence, from this place – to the Tower.

DUDLEY sees the pale look of fear in ELIZABETH's eyes and makes an aggressive movement towards SUSSEX.
   SUSSEX's hand hovers over his sword.
   DUDLEY turns to ELIZABETH, blocking SUSSEX's view with his body, fixing her with his gaze.

DUDLEY: Remember who you are. Don't be afraid.

He takes off the chain from around his neck and places a small medallion, with his coat of arms, the bear and ragged staff into her hand ... Her fist closes over it.

DUDLEY: God keep you, my Lady.

ELIZABETH looks up at SUSSEX and walks towards him.

Opposite: *Robert Dudley, Earl of Leicester (Joseph Fiennes)*
Above: *The Earl of Sussex (Jamie Foreman) arrives to take Elizabeth to the Tower of London*

CUT TO: INT. WYATT'S CELL, TOWER OF LONDON – DAY

The door to the cell swings open. A YOUNG MAN is stretched out on a rack, watched by SIR JOHN GAGE, Master of the Tower. The camera travels along his body revealing that he is being hideously tortured.

GAGE: Confess, Sir Thomas. Only confess …

EXT. BOAT, RIVER THAMES – EVENING

ELIZABETH, wearing only a simple white dress, stands in the boat. Her ladies, KAT ASHLEY and ISABEL KNOLLYS, sit next to her.
    KAT is crying. Torches flare in the gloom. SOLDIERS armed with crossbows are positioned on the boat, for fear of ambush.
    The massive, grey, forbidding shape of the Tower of London looms in front of them through the darkness.

CUT TO: EXT. TOWER OF LONDON – EVENING

The boat approaches the waterside gate, lit by torches fixed to spikes above it. The BOATMAN cries ahead, the boat slows …
    ELIZABETH glances up – and sees the heads of five of Wyatt's rebels, fixed to the spikes.
    For an instant her nerve fails. She grasps KAT's hand.

VOICE: Oars in. Open the gates for the prisoner!

The water gates are winched open. The boat glides through …

EXT. STEPS, TOWER OF LONDON – EVENING

Into a cavernous gloom, where the lapping water and the MEN's voices echo. The boat bumps against the quay and is tied up. A heavy swell, following, bucks it against the stone steps; covers them, then drains back to mud. Above them now are more lighted torches, and the dark silhouetted figures of ranks of SOLDIERS, and the MASTER OF THE TOWER. ARUNDEL and SUSSEX are there also.

MASTER OF THE TOWER: Prisoner to the steps!

ELIZABETH glances out and sees that no one is prepared to help her from the boat.
    As she steps out her shoes sink into the mud and water swills over the bottom of her white dress, staining it. She climbs the very steep steps, then hesitates.

SUSSEX: Come, Madam.

Suddenly she turns and sits down upon the stone steps. She sits still. ARUNDEL moves down to her.

ARUNDEL: Madam. You cannot sit here. It is not seemly.

ELIZABETH: I had rather sit here than in a worse place. For God knows what you mean to do to me.

He holds his hand out to her. She ignores it but holds her own hand out to ISABEL, who, frightened and crying, has joined her. KAT follows. They move up the steps, passing ARUNDEL and SUSSEX.

INT. TOWER OF LONDON – EVENING

ELIZABETH is escorted by ARUNDEL and SUSSEX down a narrow corridor. They stop by a closed door with a grid. A GUARD pushes KAT and ISABEL.
    The WARDEN opens the door to the cell. ELIZABETH does not move. ARUNDEL turns to her.

ARUNDEL: Madam, you are cold.

ELIZABETH: I do not need your pity.

ARUNDEL: Accept it then – for my sake.

She looks at him.

ELIZABETH: Thank you. (*ARUNDEL places the cloak round her shoulders.*) I shall not forget this kindness.

ELIZABETH enters the cell. KAT and ISABEL follow. The door shuts behind them.

CUT TO: INT. CORRIDOR, TOWER OF LONDON – EVENING

ARUNDEL turns to SUSSEX and the MASTER OF THE TOWER.

ARUNDEL: Be careful how you deal with her, my Lord. She is still a King's daughter – and we may all be answerable hereafter.

He makes his way through the GUARDS. SUSSEX catches up with ARUNDEL. He sneers at him.

SUSSEX: Have a care yourself, Lord Arundel – unless you want it supposed that you condone her treason.

SUSSEX walks away.

CUT TO: INT. WYATT'S CELL, TOWER OF LONDON – NIGHT

Pitch black. A door is unlocked, creaks open, and ELIZABETH enters, GAGE and SUSSEX behind her.

SUSSEX: Your friend, Sir Thomas Wyatt.

She stoops to enter and the door slams behind her. She hears a voice from the darkness.

WYATT: You should not look upon me ...

She sees WYATT crouched in a corner, badly beaten. Rats run around him. She slowly makes her way towards him.

WYATT: Each day ... I pray to God they will kill me ... but each day they do not ... only ... hurt me more ...

ELIZABETH moves closer and leans down towards him.

WYATT: And all ... all they ever ask is ... will I confess ... confess to the guilt ... and ... complicity of ... the Lady Elizabeth ... ?

WYATT breaks down, crying, and then continues.

WYATT: And ... if I will, they ... they promise ... they swear ... to put an end to my ... agonies ...

WYATT starts to weep, horribly, like a soul in torment. His filthy hand stretches out to her. ELIZABETH finally takes hold of it.

ELIZABETH: And ... will you, Thomas? Thomas ... Thomas ... will you?

CUT TO: INT. INTERROGATION CHAMBER, TOWER OF LONDON – DAY

ELIZABETH sits in the middle of the room surrounded by GARDINER, SUSSEX, ARUNDEL and another MAN.
She looks exhausted, she is wilting, they have been going at her for some time. They pace around her as they question her.

GARDINER: ... And you replied to these letters?

ELIZABETH: I cannot confess to something I did not do.

SUSSEX: Your denials are all in vain.

GARDINER: You knew of the rebellion, Madam. You were party to it. It is plain enough.

ELIZABETH: Where is your proof?

SUSSEX: But it was all to your advantage!

ELIZABETH: You must let me see the Queen. Let me speak with her.

GARDINER: You despise the Queen and the Catholic faith.

ELIZABETH: I am a true and faithful subject. I attend Mass. I ...

GARDINER: You pretend! But in your heart ...

ELIZABETH, distraught, lowers her face, mumbles something.

SUSSEX: What's that? What say you, Madam? Speak up!

ARUNDEL: Madam, if there is some small truth to these charges, however innocently and unknowingly you did proceed – then you had best confess and ...

ELIZABETH looks up, tears brimming in her eyes.

ELIZABETH: I ask you why we must tear ourselves apart for this small question of religion … Catholic, Protestant …

GARDINER: You think it small?! Though it killed your mother!

She stares at him.

ELIZABETH: We all believe in one God, my Lords.

ARUNDEL *(gently)*: No, Madam. For one is true belief – the other … heresy.

CUT TO: INT. A BORDELLO, PARIS – NIGHT

In the soft glow of candlelight we see the face of a beautiful YOUNG MAN. He is smiling. Now we see, next to him, two young women, watching the hands of an OLDER MAN, whose own face is lost in shadow: SIR FRANCIS WALSINGHAM.
   The YOUNG MAN smiles again as WALSINGHAM touches his face, caressingly – and a playing card mysteriously appears in his hand: the Jack of Spades.

WALSINGHAM: Regardez! … Le pauvre valet: un jeune homme courageux … imprudent, impétueux, naïf …
   [Look! The poor knave: a young, brave, foolish fellow, impetuous, unworldly …]

WALSINGHAM laughs, softly, leans forward a little, and the light catches his intense, compelling face.

YOUNG MAN: … Mais beau … gentil … et tendre.
   [… but beautiful … kind … and loving.]

A dark hand appears, touches WALSINGHAM's face, and turns it towards a beautiful, black GIRL who is sitting on his other side. Now he caresses her.

WALSINGHAM: Hélas! Voyez comme il est facilement dupé par la Reine noire!
   [Alas! See how easily he is trumped by the dark Queen!]

Another card appears magically in his hand: the Queen of Spades. The GIRL smiles, as he places it across the Jack. But then WALSINGHAM once more transfers his gaze and promiscuous attentions, this time to another YOUNG WOMAN, this one blonde, but equally beautiful. He touches her sensually. The Queen of Spades tries to entice him back. She begins undressing.

WALSINGHAM: Voilà!

He extracts a card, the Queen of Hearts, placing it beside the Queen of Spades.

WALSINGHAM: Mais elle est impuissante. Elle n'est pas protégée. Que peut-elle faire?
[But she is powerless. She is unprotected. What can she do?]

Another YOUNG MAN now slips quietly into the room: THOMAS ELYOT. WALSINGHAM glances over at him. ELYOT whispers to WALSINGHAM and leaves. Then WALSINGHAM turns back to the table.

WALSINGHAM (cont'd): Peut-être que sa main n'ést pas aussi vide après tout.
[Perhaps her hand is not so empty, after all.]

He produces the Ace of Spades and places it over the Queen of Spades.

CUT TO: INT. MARY'S BEDCHAMBER, WHITEHALL PALACE – NIGHT

MARY sits alone, her knees drawn up to her chin, moaning and rocking constantly back and forth, back and forth … Her DWARF tries to comfort her. MARY suddenly pushes her away. We pull back wide – and now see, at the far end of the room, a group of PHYSICIANS, DOCTORS and LADIES, including LETTICE. They watch the QUEEN in appalled silence, as she runs to and kneels below a statue of the Virgin Mary. LETTICE slips out.

INT. MARY'S PRIVY CHAMBERS, WHITEHALL PALACE – NIGHT

LETTICE hurries out of the Privy Chambers – to find the court crowded with people in a visible state of alarm and excitement, and awash with rumour. LETTICE pushes her way between them. She finds NORFOLK. She whispers in his ear.

COURTIERS watch, whisper, speculate as NORFOLK pushes his way through to the doors of the Privy Chambers.

Sir Francis Walsingham (Geoffrey Rush)

INT. OUTSIDE ELIZABETH'S CELL, BELL TOWER – NIGHT

The MASTER OF THE TOWER arrives with two GUARDS to the door of ELIZABETH's cell.

Through the grid – ELIZABETH waits – flanked on either side by KAT and ISABEL. Hearing the footsteps approach, ELIZABETH reacts.

ELIZABETH: Tonight I think to die!

The MASTER OF THE TOWER hustles ELIZABETH out of her cell. KAT is held back by SOLDIERS. She is screaming.

KAT: No, No!

As ELIZABETH is escorted down the corridor, KAT cries out.

KAT: God be with you, my Lady!

The door to the cell slams shut.

EXT. TRAITOR'S GATE – NIGHT

ELIZABETH sits in a carriage. Outside there is an air of chaos. Through the window of the carriage we glimpse SOLDIERS running to and fro.

INT. MARY'S BEDCHAMBER, WHITEHALL PALACE – NIGHT

A door behind a tapestry opens. ELIZABETH appears alone now. She walks into this dark, strange, disquieting world of icons, shrines and burning candles …

ELIZABETH falls to her knees, sensing a presence but not seeing anyone in the room.

ELIZABETH: I am your Majesty's most humble servant.

Then MARY appears – struggling to hold herself erect against the pain – cadaverous, pale as death, her eyes blazing with a kind of madness.

MARY crosses the room, accompanied by her female DWARF. She picks up a document. Then sits in a chair.

MARY: Come here!

ELIZABETH rises, moves closer.

MARY *(cont'd)*: Closer! … so I might see your face!

Closer. MARY stares at her, into her eyes.

MARY: When I look at you, I see nothing of the King – only that whore, your mother. My father never did anything so well, as to remove her head.

We see a flash of pain behind ELIZABETH's eyes.

ELIZABETH: Your Majesty forgets, he was also my father.

A flash of anger behind MARY's eyes.

MARY: Why will you not confess your crimes against me?

ELIZABETH: Because, your Majesty, I have committed none.

MARY: You speak with such sincerity.
(A beat) I see you are still a consummate actress.

She puts her hand to her stomach with a look of deepest anguish.

MARY (cont'd): They have poisoned my child. They say it is a tumour. But they are lying!
(A beat) My husband is gone.
(She gets up and paces by her throne.) I am abandoned by both God and men …

She starts to weep.

MARY: I did not burn those people to punish them – only to save them!

The pain – the human pain – in her face is so great that ELIZABETH starts to reach out towards her.

ELIZABETH: Madam, you are not well.

MARY looks at her – and the expression changes again. She shrieks out.

MARY: Do not pity me! They say this cancer will make you Queen – but they are wrong!

She moves back to the desk, on which there is the document.

MARY: Look there! It is your death warrant. All I need do is sign it!

ELIZABETH (kneeling before her): Mary, if you sign that paper you will be murdering your own sister.

She stares at her. Suddenly with grotesque energy, MARY grasps her wrist and puts her face close to ELIZABETH.

MARY: You will promise me something. When I am gone, you will do everything in your power to uphold the Catholic faith. Do not take away from the people the consolations of the Blessed Virgin, their Holy Mother.

ELIZABETH: When I am Queen, I promise to act as my conscience dictates.

MARY interrupts her furiously, savagely, and jumps up.

MARY: Do not think to be Queen at all – for I am not going to die! You may return to Hatfield.

She sits on throne.

MARY *(cont'd)*: But you will remain under arrest, until I am recovered.

ELIZABETH curtseys low.

ELIZABETH: Thank you, your Majesty …

ELIZABETH prepares to slip out through the side door.

MARY: No. Feed her to the wolves! Let her see what they are like!

The DWARF escorts ELIZABETH to the main doors. As they approach them, ELIZABETH can hear loud and hectic noises on the other side … the sound of a court convulsed with panic and desperate with rumour. The DWARF opens the door, and follows ELIZABETH out.

INT. COURT, WHITEHALL PALACE – NIGHT

The court is packed. As ELIZABETH appears, accompanied by Mary's DWARF, they all fall silent. ELIZABETH looks around at the sea of faces … moves forward hesitantly, unsure … The DWARF watches her.
 ELIZABETH bows to the court. She gets up and walks down through the hushed COURTIERS. They wait for her to say something. She begins hesitantly.

ELIZABETH: I … I have … just visited with the … with the Queen, my … my sister. She suffers much, but finds comfort in her faith … we must all pray for her most complete recovery.

There are murmurs of assent. ELIZABETH walks, as regally as she can manage, through them … her face composed … but as she passes through to the corridor she is visibly relieved.
 ELIZABETH is startled by a COURTIER, who appears out of the dark, and whispers furtively

COURTIER: Madam – you must take confession before you leave!

She looks at him, confused.

ELIZABETH: Confession? Of course.

The COURTIER melts away. NORFOLK strides through the court, accompanied by SUSSEX.

NORFOLK *(To one of his MEN)*: She is just a child yet still you piss yourselves!

NORFOLK'S MAN: Your Grace, Protestants are already returning from abroad …

NORFOLK: Yes, yes, and have made plans to massacre every Catholic in England!
(Sarcastic) There would be butchery indeed …

NORFOLK'S MAN: They say Walsingham will return from France …

NORFOLK: Walsingham is nothing.

He walks away, past another of his MEN, who walks with him.

NORFOLK *(low, to the other MAN)*: Be sure he does not.

He continues up the stairs towards the Bedchamber. SUSSEX falls in with him.

SUSSEX *(low)*: Perhaps your Grace should consider another expediency.

NORFOLK keeps walking.

SUSSEX: Go yourself to France. Make alliance with Mary of Scots, and by means of it … remove this bastard woman, and make … a better King.

NORFOLK stops, and reacts with a kind of cold stare. Their faces are inches apart.

NORFOLK: Do you not know that the price of treason is death, my Lord? As is the price of suggesting it.

SUSSEX watches him go.

INT. CONFESSION BOX – EVENING

ELIZABETH sits in the darkness. After a few moments she hears the "PRIEST" on the other side.

"PRIEST" *(V.O.)*: In nomine Patris, et Filii, et Spiritus Sancti …

ELIZABETH: Father, I have searched my heart as humbly as I can and I have found nothing to confess.

The "PRIEST" opens the small grille between them, and ELIZABETH has a glimpse of his face: grizzled, strong, with a trimmed white beard: SIR WILLIAM CECIL.

ELIZABETH: Sir William! …

CECIL: Are you well?

ELIZABETH: As well as can be expected …

CECIL: There was nowhere else we could meet in safety.
(A beat) You must listen to me carefully! All things move in our favour. Many of our friends are even now returning from exile.
(A beat) But these are still most uncertain times, and your life is still in danger. You must say nothing, meet no one whose visit may compromise you.

ELIZABETH: No one?

CECIL: No one! Not even Lord Robert.

She stares at him, shakes her head.

ELIZABETH: He is a trusted friend.

CECIL *(impatient)*: Child, listen to me, please! You are most innocent in the ways of this world … and we must do all we may to guarantee the security of your throne.
(A beat) There is one person whom I do wish you to speak to.

ELIZABETH stares at him.

CECIL: Monseigneur Alvaro de la Quadra – the Spanish Ambassador.

ELIZABETH: Sir William, I am not prepared to …

Before ELIZABETH has a chance to protest, CECIL has gone. Suddenly she catches a glimpse of ALVARO's face through the grille.

ALVARO: My Lady … I bring a message. The King of Spain is enraptured and offers you his hand in marriage.

A beat. ELIZABETH is shocked.

ELIZABETH: My sister is not yet dead. Her bed is still warm.

ALVARO: His Majesty finds it already cold.

CUT TO: INT. MARY'S BEDCHAMBER, WHITEHALL PALACE – NIGHT

We see a statue of the Virgin Mary & Child, built into a column.
    NORFOLK enters. MARY is lying on the bed, breathless. LETTICE and other LADIES are in attendance. NORFOLK strides over to the desk, picks up the death warrant and a seal, and puts the warrant in front of MARY.

NORFOLK: You must sign it!

She does not respond.

NORFOLK: For the love of God! Sign it!

MARY ignores him and turns away to face the DWARF, who strokes her head.

NORFOLK *(in frustration)*: Will you leave your Kingdom to a heretic!?

MARY covers her ears with her hands, and takes comfort in the DWARF.

Elizabeth takes confession

INT. CHAMBERS, PARIS – DAY

WALSINGHAM is sitting on his bed, musing.

WALSINGHAM: And yet, when you look around, there is so little beauty in this world – and so much suffering. Do you suppose that is what God had in mind?

Across the room a YOUNG MAN is looking at one of WALSINGHAM's books
He starts to walk casually towards WALSINGHAM.

WALSINGHAM: That is to say – if there is a God at all.

As he speaks, the YOUNG MAN moves behind WALSINGHAM and draws a knife.

WALSINGHAM *(cont'd)*: … Perhaps there is nothing in this universe but ourselves … and our thoughts …

With a sudden movement the YOUNG MAN presses the knife to WALSINGHAM's throat. WALSINGHAM does not react.

WALSINGHAM *(cont'd)*: Why are you trembling?

The YOUNG MAN's hand trembles.

YOUNG MAN: Vous êtes Walsingham!

WALSINGHAM still does not react.

WALSINGHAM: Think before you do this … Do not take yourself away from my protection – for after it is done they will surely kill you.

Sensing the YOUNG MAN's uncertainty, WALSINGHAM sits up on the edge of the bed to face the YOUNG MAN, but the knife is still at his neck.

WALSINGHAM: If you must, do it now and without regret. But first think carefully and be certain that it needs must be done.

The YOUNG MAN's hand wavers. Slowly, WALSINGHAM stands up and puts his hand on the YOUNG MAN's arm and touches his head.

WALSINGHAM: Viens ici!

WALSINGHAM walks away to the window. The YOUNG MAN lowers the knife, stands and follows him across to the window.
WALSINGHAM opens the window. Paris stretches out below them.

WALSINGHAM *(cont'd)*: Look out there! There is a whole world waiting for you. A sorry but magnificent world. There is much to strive for. Innocence is the most precious thing you possess. Lose it, and you lose your soul.

The confusion in the YOUNG MAN's eyes turns to something else: a smile, a confidence. He seems mesmerised. Looking at that radiant face with the same deep compassion and understanding, WALSINGHAM cuts his throat.

INT. CHAMBERS, HATFIELD HOUSE – DAY

Several GUARDS are seated at a table. They look across to ELIZABETH and DUDLEY, who are apparently engaged in an innocent game of backgammon. As they move the pieces, their hands brush against each other.

ELIZABETH *(whispers)*: He then said this King would marry me, but would not expect to share my bed more than two or three times a year … ?!

DUDLEY *(after a beat)*: As much as that?

She glances at him and sees he is smiling, teasing her.

ELIZABETH: Well, he is enraptured …

DUDLEY: Naturally …

ELIZABETH: … But his affairs would otherwise keep him in Spain.

Their laughter has alerted the GUARDS, who look across. They fall quiet.

DUDLEY *(lower)*: Then the King is a fool! For what affairs could ever be important enough to keep him from your bed?

ELIZABETH suppresses a smile.

ELIZABETH: Robert, you should not say such things.

DUDLEY: Then I will only think them.

A guard crosses the room, then rejoins the others at the table.

ELIZABETH: Please do not tease me, Robert. Everything is so uncertain. Sir William says I have many enemies, and my life is still in danger.

DUDLEY: Do not listen to everything Sir William Cecil tells you. Do not listen to any of them! None of them is of consequence. When you are Queen …

ELIZABETH: … I am not Queen yet …

DUDLEY: You will be. Elizabeth, Queen of England. A court to worship you, a country to obey you … poems written to celebrate your beauty, music composed in your honour. And all of these people … They will be nothing to you.
(A beat) I will mean nothing to you.

Suddenly she begins to laugh, which alerts the GUARDS, who look across.

ELIZABETH: You mean everything to me! Our love fills every space, every vacancy!

They stare at each other. Then DUDLEY's expression changes to a teasing smile.

ELIZABETH: My eyes …

DUDLEY: All of what I am. It is you.

Their eyes lock.

ABOVE: *The Duke of Norfolk (Christopher Ecclestone) removes Mary's ring*

INT. MARY'S BEDCHAMBER, WHITEHALL PALACE – DAY

MARY lies on her death bed, barely breathing. A PRIEST administers the last rites.

PRIEST: Ave Maria, gratia plena, Dominus tecum. Benedicta tu in mulieribus, et benedictus fructus ventris tui, Iesus. Sancta Maria, Mater Dei, ora pro nobis peccatoribus, nunc, et in hora mortis nostrae. Amen.

MARY is heard to gasp, then grows silent. NORFOLK is standing by the bed. The PRIEST continues to administer the last rites. Then he stops – pauses – puts his head close to MARY's mouth. He nods to NORFOLK.

NORFOLK: Is she dead?

Without compunction, NORFOLK pulls the coronation ring right off her finger. He gives it to SUSSEX.

NORFOLK: Give it to her!

Close on the ring in Sussex's hand.

CUT TO: EXT. LONDON CHURCH – DAY

The church bells begin to toll for Mary's death. Gradually we hear, then see, other bells joining in. We pull back until we see the whole of London, which seems to be filled with their noise.

CUT TO: INT. CORRIDOR/CHAMBERS, HATFIELD HOUSE – DAY

KAT, ISABEL, and other LADIES hurry through the corridors of the house, excited ... the bells tolling, loudly in the background. KAT rushes towards ELIZABETH, who sits alone.

KAT *(excited)***:** My Lady, the Earl of Sussex is here.

ELIZABETH composes herself, then rises and moves into the bright sunlight of the garden. Her LADIES follow.

CUT TO: EXT. GARDEN, HATFIELD – DAY

SUSSEX is waiting for her.

SUSSEX: The Queen is dead.
(He falls to his knees.) Long live the Queen!

He holds out his hand. The ring sits in the palm of it. ELIZABETH's hand moves slowly to take the ring ... she takes it. SUSSEX backs away, and rejoins his men.

ALL: Long live the Queen! Long live the Queen!

ELIZABETH: This is the Lord's doing and it is marvellous in our eyes.

THE SCRIPT : 41

CUT TO: INT. WESTMINSTER ABBEY – DAY

A circling image of a gold-studded ceiling.

NORFOLK *(V.O.)*: To the North …

Cut to close on the Queen's crown held up in NORFOLK's hands.

NORFOLK: … I present on to you Elizabeth, your undoubted Queen.

Cut to close on NORFOLK.

NORFOLK: To the South, I present on to you Elizabeth, your undoubted Queen.

Cut to a scene of magnificent medieval pageantry: the great Abbey packed to the rafters, the PEERS and PEER-ESSES in their glorious robes, glittering with jewels.
    ELIZABETH moves to the throne, wearing the tunic of gold, her flowing robe held by her LADIES-IN-WAITING. She sits on the throne. Behind the throne stand the great nobles of England: NORFOLK, DERBY, ARUNDEL, HOWARD, SUSSEX holding their coronets …
    ELIZABETH's face is impassive. The BISHOP OF

CARLISLE raises the crown high over her head.

BISHOP: I crown thee Elizabeth, Queen of England, Ireland, and France. God save your Majesty!

He places the crown upon ELIZABETH's head. He takes the sceptre from SUSSEX and hands it to her. He then turns to ARUNDEL and takes the orb, which he places in ELIZABETH's hand.
    The great LORDS put on their own coronets, the silver trumpets blow and drums beat, cannons roar outside. The crowds shout out: "Long live the Queen! Long live the Queen!" The CHOIR begins to sing "Tallis Te Deum", the organ to play, and all together the noise is "like unto the end of the world!".

EXT. WESTMINSTER ABBEY – DAY

As ELIZABETH emerges into the light, a huge CROWD of people acclaim her with resounding, almost deafening cheers. Overwhelmed by the sight and the sound of it, she smiles …

CECIL *(V.O.)*: Your Majesty should know that you have inherited a most parlous and degenerate state …

Above: *Elizabeth is crowned*

Opposite top: *Behind the scenes*

Opposite bottom: *Outside Westminster Abbey*

Above: *Cecil (Richard Attenborough)*
Opposite, far right: *Waad (Angus Deayton)*

CUT TO: INT. ELIZABETH'S BEDCHAMBER – DAY

ELIZABETH is divested of her robes, aided by her LADIES-IN-WAITING, and the precious crown jewels, which, with the orb and sceptre and the swords of state, are placed in iron cases. CECIL, WAAD and other COURTIERS stand formally by.

CECIL: Your Majesty should know that you have inherited a most parlous and degenerate state. It is threatened from abroad by the ambitions of France and Spain – but is weaker in strength, men, money and riches than I have ever known it …

ELIZABETH looks at him uneasily.

ELIZABETH: What are you saying?

CECIL glances at WAAD, encouraging him to speak.

WAAD: Madam, your treasury is empty. The navy is run down. There is no standing army and we are bare of munitions. And there is not a fortress left in England which could withstand a single shot.

ELIZABETH: I have no desire to go to war, Sir.

CECIL: But nor is that the end of it. Apart from abroad, there are those, both here and abroad, who wish your Majesty ill. Mary of Scots has already laid claim to your throne, and Norfolk … Norfolk covets it relentlessly. Madam, until you marry and produce an heir you will not find security.

She looks back at him.

CUT TO: INT. GREAT HALL, WHITEHALL PALACE – NIGHT

ELIZABETH sits on her throne. She watches DUDLEY dancing – sees how easily he flirts with the young and beautiful WOMEN around him, and how eagerly they respond. To one side of her are her young and beautiful MAIDS OF HONOUR, including KAT and ISABEL. On her other side is SIR WILLIAM CECIL.
    DUDLEY gives a look to ELIZABETH.
    Another P.O.V. – through a red net and candles. (This is Walsingham's P.O.V. – but we do not yet see him.)
    High above the court and looking down on it, we see the dancing and ELIZABETH on the throne. CECIL introduces a number of YOUNG MEN to her.
    ELIZABETH takes scant notice of the men being introduced as KAT whispers to her.

KAT: That is John Harrington …

CECIL: Sir John Spencer, Madam.

KAT *(cont'd)*: … They say he's a great scholar.

ELIZABETH looks across to him.

ELIZABETH *(laughs)*: Too skinny! I think he reads too many books.

CECIL: Henry Marks.

ELIZABETH *(after a beat)*: Who is that? …

CECIL *(interrupting)*: Master Robin Brown from Nottingham.

A beautiful YOUNG MAN with masses of dark curls and long shapely legs.

KAT: … That is Sir Christopher Hatton.

KAT whispers something. ELIZABETH, amused, appraises him. The YOUNG MAN notices her attention and bows.

ELIZABETH: Pity, he has nice legs.

They suppress their laughter.

ELIZABETH *(cont'd, lightly)*: I do not see why I should marry at all.

CECIL: Lord Ensley, Madam.

ELIZABETH stands.

KAT: But Madam, they say that when spinsters die they are sent to hell and forced to couple with apes there.

ISABEL: What is the difference? They have to do it in this life, too!

They laugh. ELIZABETH glances round, then, accompanied by CECIL and her LADIES-IN-WAITING, she walks through the court. COURTIERS sink to their knees in front of her. She smiles readily, offering her hand to some.
    A new dance starts. DUDLEY dances amid the men as they face and flirt with the women dancing opposite. Rose petals float down from above.
    Again we see ELIZABETH through the red net curtain. This time we see WALSINGHAM as he watches her. She glances up and catches him looking at her.
    ELIZABETH moves on – again watching DUDLEY dancing. CECIL continues to present COURTIERS to ELIZABETH. Suddenly ALVARO appears, blocking her way.

CECIL: You will recall his Excellency, the Spanish Ambassador.

ALVARO bows deeply.

ELIZABETH: How could I forget? Excellency.

She holds out her hand, for him to kiss.

ALVARO: Your Majesty.

ELIZABETH moves on and ALVARO backs off. He moves through the dancers to join NORFOLK, surrounded by his supporters including ELYOT, SUSSEX and LETTICE.
    The DANCERS dance around ELIZABETH. She notices a man watching her. She turns to CECIL.

ELIZABETH: Do I know that gentleman?

CECIL: Oh, that is Sir Francis Walsingham. The gentleman of whom we spoke. He has returned from exile now, and I have appointed him to have a care for your Majesty's person.

The camera moves in close on ELIZABETH as she looks at WALSINGHAM.
    CECIL sees DE FOIX nearby and goes to him. ELIZABETH stares back at WALSINGHAM. He has gone … At that moment DUDLEY dances up to her, then skips off as CECIL brings DE FOIX across to meet her.

CECIL: Majesty, Majesty. May I introduce the French Ambassador, his Excellency, Monsieur de Foix.

ELIZABETH tears her eyes away from DUDLEY to see a tall, handsome Frenchman. He bows.

Above: *Monsieur de Foix (Eric Cantona) is introduced to Elizabeth*
Opposite: *Director Shekhar Kapur on violin*

ELIZABETH: Excellency.

She offers her hand. DE FOIX kisses it and looks into her eyes. She smiles and DE FOIX smiles in return.

DE FOIX: King Henry of Anjou sends you his brotherly love. He trusts that, with your accession, the relationship between our countries may be much improved.

ELIZABETH: That is also my hope.

She looks over at DUDLEY again, dancing.

DE FOIX: With such consideration, the King expects that you will consider the suit of his brother, the Duke of Anjou.

CECIL interrupts.

CECIL: Her Majesty will naturally consider the proposal most carefully.

ELIZABETH turns to DE FOIX.
Cut to NORFOLK and ALVARO watching the exchange with interest.

NORFOLK: I suppose the French do offer some suitor to her!

ALVARO: Naturally. Everything now depends upon the husband that woman takes!

Cut to ELIZABETH, DE FOIX and CECIL.

ELIZABETH: It is unfortunate, however, that at this time the Duke's aunt, Mary of Guise, chooses to garrison Scotland with French troops.

DE FOIX, and CECIL, seem for a moment equally discomfited.

DE FOIX: You would not deny, Madam, that your cousin, Mary of Scots, is the rightful Sovereign of that poor country?

ELIZABETH: I would not … and you, Sir, would not deny that my cousin is not the rightful sovereign of this "poor country"?

She calls to her LADIES, who follow her off. CECIL guides DE FOIX away.

CECIL: Her Majesty does not deny it.

Cut to WALSINGHAM slowly weaving his way through the dancers. NORFOLK notices WALSINGHAM moving towards them. He does not bat an eyelid. Arriving, WALSINGHAM bows.

WALSINGHAM: Your Grace …

NORFOLK: Walsingham. Welcome to England.

WALSINGHAM smiles and looks into his eyes.

WALSINGHAM: Your Grace is surprised?

NORFOLK recovers himself, shakes his head.

NORFOLK: No. Only – a little disappointed.

He moves forward, away from WALSINGHAM, with his people including ALVARO and SUSSEX following in his wake. WALSINGHAM notices LETTICE is about to go with him but hesitates. WALSINGHAM catches her eye – and smiles.

ELIZABETH finally moves towards the DANCERS. They stop, fall to their knees and the music ceases. She walks over to DUDLEY, taps his shoulder, and turns to the MUSICIANS.

ELIZABETH *(to MUSICIANS)*: Play a volta!

DUDLEY bows. She looks over at the MUSICIANS, who strike up again. The rest of the court draws back, so that they may dance alone. As part of the dance DUDLEY has to grasp her around the waist and throw her high into the air, then catch her as she falls. He does this so athletically that there are audible gasps, and applause, from the audience …
NORFOLK watches them. DUDLEY throws ELIZABETH high in the air, catches her in his arms.

DUDLEY *(sotto)*: When may I see you – in private?

She laughs.

ELIZABETH *(sotto)*: In private? … Have you forgot, my Lord? I am Queen now.

He looks at her then throws her high into the air again, controlling her movements, leaving ELIZABETH breathless.

Above and
opposite: *Elizabeth
and Dudley scandalise
the court with their
dancing*

Above : *Elizabeth's Ladies-in-Waiting*

CUT TO: INT. OUTSIDE ELIZABETH'S BEDCHAMBER, WHITEHALL – NIGHT

The Queen's DWARF runs into the corridor bustling with excitement. ISABEL and KAT are peeping into the Queen's bedchamber.

DWARF: He's coming.

ISABEL: He's coming.

A flurry of movement, as the LADIES line up in the corridor. DUDLEY enters, then stops as he sees them.

DUDLEY: Ah …

He walks on past them.

DUDLEY: My Ladies.

LADIES: My Lord.

He stops by ISABEL.

DUDLEY: You blush, my Lady Knollys. Are you in love?

ISABEL: No, my Lord.

DUDLEY: Then you should be – or waste all that beauty.

He moves on past KAT, who frowns at him as he walks past into the Queen's bedchamber. KAT sweeps away.

KAT: Come on, Ladies, that is enough now. Isabel.

The LADIES peep into the room, giggling.

INT. ELIZABETH'S BEDCHAMBER, WHITEHALL PALACE – NIGHT

DUDLEY enters the room, looking through the metal screen. He crosses the candlelit room. There is no sign of ELIZABETH.
We catch a glimpse of him through silk drapes, as he passes the bed to find ELIZABETH curled up beside the bed. DUDLEY sits near to her.

ELIZABETH: My Lord …

DUDLEY: Your Majesty …

INT. OUTSIDE ELIZABETH'S BEDCHAMBER, WHITEHALL PALACE – NIGHT

ISABEL and several of the other LADIES are standing around looking through the holes into the Queen's bedchamber.

YOUNG LADY: But they are laughing!

KAT enters the corridor.

KAT: You ought not to look! Come away from there!

The LADIES ignore her and KAT joins in, looking through to the room.

INT. ELIZABETH'S BEDCHAMBER, WHITEHALL PALACE – NIGHT

DUDLEY sits near to ELIZABETH, the sheer drapes of the bed brushing against them. They look at one another.

ELIZABETH: What are you looking at?

DUDLEY: I wondered … if you were different?

ELIZABETH: How different?

DUDLEY: Now you are Queen.

ELIZABETH: Do I not have the same face? … The same … feelings?

DUDLEY *(slightly teasing)*: Do you?

ELIZABETH: How shall I prove it to you?

DUDLEY *(soft)*: Like this.

CUT TO: INT. OUTSIDE ELIZABETH'S BEDCHAMBER, WHITEHALL PALACE – NIGHT

The LADIES are interrupted by the sound of a door opening, and then footsteps. They quickly move away from the wall as CECIL appears. They curtsey – but try not to catch his eye. He senses something is wrong.

CECIL: Does her Majesty sleep?

ISABEL: Not … yet, Sir William. She is … overwrought.

Some of the others try to suppress their giggles. A few turn bright red. CECIL notices and frowns. CECIL stands his ground, looks at them.

CECIL: I wish you to show me her Majesty's sheets every morning. I must know all her proper functions.

KAT tries to keep a straight face.

KAT: Her … proper … functions … Sir William?

ISABEL and some of the others try not to snort with laughter. CECIL regards them coldly.

CECIL: Indeed. Her Majesty's body and person are no longer her own property. They belong to the state.

KAT *(sober)*: Yes, Sir William.

They curtsey as CECIL stalks out of the chamber. They then all collapse with giggles and turn to look into the bedchamber once more.

INT. ELIZABETH'S BEDCHAMBER, WHITEHALL PALACE – NIGHT

ELIZABETH and DUDLEY make love on the bed, half undressed, but covered, wrapped, and moving within the sensuous flow of satin. They whisper … half-heard voices softly echoing.

CUT TO: INT. CHAPEL, ST PETER'S, ROME – DAY

In the small chapel, the seventy-year-old PONTIFF, wearing a white skullcap, is blessing some angelic-looking CHILDREN. Several PRIESTS stand watching.

POPE: Benedicite, omnia opera Domini, Domino.

As he moves to the next boy, a red-robed CARDINAL whispers something to him. The POPE looks in the direction of a young English priest, BALLARD. The POPE sits on his throne and gestures to BALLARD to join him. BALLARD kisses the POPE's ring.

POPE: Tell me, my son, what news of our brothers and sisters in England? Do they accept the sovereignty of that illegitimate whore?

BALLARD: No, Holy Father, they pray ceaselessly that England may be recovered from heresy.

POPE: Perhaps prayers may not be sufficient. I will ask for guidance, in this matter. But do not despair, for it is truly said that the righteous shall inherit the earth.

He smiles, then abruptly stands and walks back to the CHILDREN.

EXT. BARREN LANDSCAPE – DUSK

Three silhouetted HORSEMEN gallop wildly across the skyline.

INT. ELIZABETH'S BEDCHAMBER, WHITEHALL PALACE – NIGHT

The crack of THUNDER. A storm breaks over the palace, with great violence. The bedchamber is filled with women – MAIDS OF HONOUR and LADIES OF THE BEDCHAMBER – as ELIZABETH is prepared for bed.

ELIZABETH stands in the middle of the room while KAT orchestrates her undressing. ELIZABETH does nothing herself.

KAT pulls back her plaits and removes her outer gown, which is carefully taken away. ISABEL joins KAT, and as they carefully hold out ELIZABETH'S hands, her rings are removed. A bowl of warm water is presented to her. Her fingers are dipped into it. ISABEL carefully dries them. Another LADY anoints her other hand.

KAT takes her place behind the QUEEN and runs her hands soothingly, sensually around her body.

The storm rages outside.

INT. ELIZABETH'S PRIVY CHAMBER, WHITEHALL PALACE – DAWN

NORFOLK strides through an empty chamber. SERVANTS at work. A CHAMBERLAIN tries to stop him.

CHAMBERLAIN: Your Grace! Your Grace! Her Majesty is not yet risen!

NORFOLK ignores him and continues on past the GUARDS towards the bedchamber.

The Pope (John Gielgud)

CUT TO: INT. ELIZABETH'S BEDCHAMBER, WHITEHALL PALACE – DAWN

NORFOLK strides in. Inside the chamber, we see KAT preparing the Queen's toilet along with two other LADIES. NORFOLK pulls back the curtain around the bed.

NORFOLK: Madam!

ELIZABETH's eyes open. She sits up.

NORFOLK *(cont'd)*: You had best get up. There is some grave news.

She looks back at him.

INT. ELIZABETH'S PRIVY CHAMBERS, WHITEHALL PALACE – MORNING

ELIZABETH still tousled from sleep, in chamber with her COUNCIL. She looks around at them.

NORFOLK: Mary of Guise has increased the French garrison in Scotland by 4,000 men.

DUDLEY enters and takes a seat.

SUSSEX: Perhaps more.

She looks at CECIL. He is grave, pained.

CECIL: Madam, Madam, I am afraid the French mean to attack while we are still weak, and while your Majesty's reign is still uncertain.

ELIZABETH, shocked, looks round at her COUNCIL.

ELIZABETH: What is your counsel?

NORFOLK *(before CECIL can reply)*: Madam, we must with all haste raise an army to march upon Scotland.

There are murmurs of assent.

ELIZABETH: Can we not send emissaries, to … ?

NORFOLK: There is no time for that! As Queen, we look to you for action … unless you are content to wait for the French to send more reinforcements.

ELIZABETH: Are you all in agreement?

SUSSEX: I say there has never been a better time or occasion to abate the French pride!

She looks at ARUNDEL.

ELIZABETH: Arundel?

ARUNDEL: War is a sin … but sometimes it is a necessary one.

She looks at DUDLEY, who seems uncomfortable and undecided.

Arundel (Edwarde Hardwicke)

DUDLEY: I …

NORFOLK: Lord Robert! You were appointed to Council to protect the interests of England! Now it appears you do not have the stomach for it!

DUDLEY: I am in agreement with Your Grace – if her Majesty's throne is at risk.

ELIZABETH becomes aware of WALSINGHAM, seated at a table near by.

ELIZABETH: And what say you, Walsingham?

SUSSEX: Your Majesty!

WALSINGHAM: Madam, I say … a prince should rather be slow to take action, and should watch that he does not come to be afraid of his own shadow.

CECIL *(hotly)*: With your permission, Madam: you are not, Sir Francis, a member of council, nor are you indeed in the majority.

WALSINGHAM says no more. ELIZABETH seems to agonise.

ELIZABETH: I do not like wars. They have uncertain outcomes.

NORFOLK: Your Majesty has no choice – as you value your throne. We must have war!

CUT TO: EXT. LEITH CASTLE, SCOTLAND – DAWN

The camera is tight on the shifting, glassy surface of a river. The first cold rays of the morning sun pierce the blue waters, which shimmer hazily.

One word appears on the screen: SCOTLAND.

Slowly, the colour changes, as if the sun were turning the blue waters red. But, as the red deepens, and the whole river is thick with it, we realise it is blood. The river is running blood. Something that looks like the fingers of a human hand poke just clear of the surface – rigid as stone.

Then other BODIES … more and more, face down, floating slackly in the thick red tide. The camera moves up … to see the BODIES snarled into a huge jam of corpses, where the river narrows. The BODIES pile up, cold, stiff as timbers, washed with blood.

The camera moves up, over a rise – to show the open, raw landscape of Scotland in the morning light, and the castle, with the flag of Mary of Guise fluttering from its ramparts in the breeze.

And on the ground between are more CORPSES – hundreds and hundreds of them, splayed grotesquely in death. A few riderless horses move among them.

Slowly we move closer to the castle … over the dead YOUNG BOYS, the trampled flags of England, the broken scaling ladders. We hear the piteous groans of the dying. FRENCH SOLDIERS move methodically, despatching them with single sword thrusts …

The slow CLIP-CLOP of hooves. From the castle MARY OF GUISE herself, clad in armour, leads a small party of her SOLDIERS, on horseback. The horses weave through the bodies. The party approaches a SOLDIER lying injured. A FRENCH SOLDIER is poised to kill him. MARY OF GUISE raises her hand to stop him. She dismounts and approaches. She kneels by the young soldier, wipes the blood from his face with her colours, which had been her coat of arms, then looks at him.

Mary of Guise (Fanny Ardant)

THE SCRIPT : 63

MARY OF GUISE: Go back to England. Take this to your Queen.

She gives him her coat of arms, then stands and turns to her SOLDIERS on horseback.

MARY OF GUISE: Renvoyez-lui chez sa Reine …
      [Take him back to his Queen …]

She gives a look back at the SOLDIER.

MARY OF GUISE *(cont'd)***:** … Et assurez-vous qu'il reste bien vivant.
      [… and make sure that he stays alive.]

The SOLDIER looks up at her.

CUT TO: INT. COURT, WHITEHALL PALACE – DAY

Camera high up looking down on ELIZABETH as she crosses below. KAT and LADIES-IN-WAITING follow. Camera still high, ELIZABETH strides angrily through the court, her LADIES trying to keep pace. The court is strangely, almost eerily empty.
   The few COURTIERS around go through the motions of bowing. She sees the palace CHAMBERLAIN.

ELIZABETH: Where are my Councillors?

CHAMBERLAIN: I know not, Madam.

She continues to stride through the empty court angrily.

ELIZABETH: Where is Lord Robert?

CHAMBERLAIN: Lord Robert is gone hunting.

ELIZABETH paces restlessly.

ELIZABETH *(to LADIES)***:** Leave me now!

KAT *(makes a moves towards her mistress)***:** Madam.

ELIZABETH: Just go! Go!

ELIZABETH strides off, leaving the LADIES-IN-WAITING.

INT. OLD CHAMBERS, WHITEHALL PALACE – DAY

ELIZABETH strides through corridors that gradually get smaller and smaller, as if closing in on her. She emerges into a huge, long-disused room. Tears of anger and humiliation well into her eyes. She sobs aloud. She is like a wounded animal … stumbling, crying, over-whelmed … And then, abruptly, she stops. Through her tears she finds herself looking at the vast, masterful portrait of her father, Henry VIII, by Holbein. She stares at it, choking back her sobs.
   The portrait shows Henry in the full flush and pomp of his power: a big, powerfully built man, his eyes flashing with arrogance, his legs planted apart. The embodiment of kingly virtues, of supreme confidence and power …
   She stares at it – then becomes conscious that, after all, she is not alone. Something makes her glance around. WALSINGHAM, standing in the shadows, is watching her – has been watching her all the time.

ELIZABETH: How dare you come into my presence? Why do you follow me here … ?

WALSINGHAM: It is my business to protect your Majesty – against all things.

ELIZABETH looks at him.

ELIZABETH: I do not need protection now. I need to be left alone.

WALSINGHAM: Majesty …

He turns to go, but stops as …

ELIZABETH: They should never have been sent to Scotland … I should have … My father would not have made such a mistake. I have been proved unfit to rule. *(She looks back at Walsingham.)* Well, that is what you all think, is it not, Walsingham?

WALSINGHAM: Madam, I am not here to judge you.

ELIZABETH: Why did they not send proper reinforcements? Why did they send such children?

WALSINGHAM: Because the bishops would not let them. They spoke against it in the pulpits.

ELIZABETH: Then – they are speaking against their Queen!

WALSINGHAM: The bishops are against you and have no fear of you. They do not expect you to survive.

ELIZABETH stares at him.

CUT TO: EXT. WOODS – DAY

DUDLEY kneels by a stag, which he has just wounded. Near by, a group of his MEN who are attending to their dogs and horses. ELIZABETH, astride a magnificent horse, *is galloping at full pace through the trees, followed by a small group of her COURTIERS.*

MAN: My Lord … the Queen!

DUDLEY looks towards ELIZABETH. ELIZABETH reins in, her horse snorting from its effort. Her COURTIERS rein in behind her. She climbs down from the saddle.

ELIZABETH: Where have you been?

She stares at him and walks away. DUDLEY follows her, not knowing what to say.

ELIZABETH: You were not at court.

DUDLEY: I was hunting.

ELIZABETH: God's death, Robert! I had need of you.

DUDLEY: I did not think that you would …

ELIZABETH: No! You did not think!

DUDLEY turns away angrily.

ELIZABETH *(cont'd)*: It is a fine beast. Let me kill it!

DUDLEY looks up at her in disbelief.

DUDLEY: For God's sake, Elizabeth!

ELIZABETH: Lord Robert, I would have the knife!

She has pulled rank. DUDLEY stands, bows and offers her the knife.

DUDLEY: Your Majesty …

She knees beside the stag and with the knife poised she looks up at DUDLEY. He stares back at her arrogantly. She raises the knife above the stag's neck and stabs downwards. The silence is disrupted by the sound of hooves. One of DUDLEY's men calls out. ELIZABETH walks over to him.

CECIL and DE FOIX appear with other riders. CECIL approaches her, panting from his exertions. He bows. DE FOIX follows.

ELIZABETH: Sir William …

CECIL: Your Majesty, Monsieur de Foix. Mary of Guise promises to make no further threat against your Majesty – but upon one condition.

ELIZABETH: What … condition?

CECIL: That your Majesty considers the proposal of her son, the Duke of Anjou.

ELIZABETH looks around for DUDLEY and crosses over near to him.

DE FOIX: The Duke is most eager to meet your Majesty. He has heard a great deal of your beauty.

CECIL moves closer to ELIZABETH, and as he does so DUDLEY moves away from her.

CECIL: For the love of God, let not the care of your diseased estate hang any longer in the balance. In marriage, and the production of an heir, lies your only surety!

DE FOIX: The Duke is also most handsome.

ELIZABETH breaks through CECIL and DE FOIX and pauses for a moment.

ELIZABETH: Very well. Invite the Duke of Anjou. We shall see him in the flesh.

DUDLEY strides off, furious and humiliated. ELIZABETH follows. DUDLEY stalks up a hill, finally coming to rest against a tree. From a distance now we watch their brief meeting – and their obvious argument. DE FOIX watches with interest.

DE FOIX: The Duke will not take kindly to a rival for his suit.

CECIL: The marriage of a Queen is borne of politics, not childish passion.

On the hillside we see DUDLEY as he makes a dismissive gesture and ELIZABETH moves away from him, coming back down the hill. Close now, we see the tears of frustration and anger in her eyes. She pauses, looks back at him, and shouts out.

ELIZABETH: … My love is not so locked up that others may never partake of it!

CUT TO: EXT. STEPS, WHITEHALL PALACE – DAY

Wonderful tents have been set up beside the river, to welcome the DUKE OF ANJOU. ELIZABETH and her COURTIERS, including DUDLEY and his MEN, await his arrival standing beneath a canopy.
They watch as the DUKE's gilded barge approaches; a HANDSOME MAN stands in the prow. Behind him MUSICIANS play. TRUMPETERS sound a fanfare of welcome.
The HANDSOME MAN walks up the hill, accompanied by the MUSICIANS. The TRUMPETERS sound another fanfare of welcome. ELIZABETH greets the HANDSOME MAN.

ELIZABETH: Enchanter …

Suddenly one of the MUSICIANS steps forward. He grabs the hat of the HANDSOME MAN.

ANJOU: Non, I am Anjou … Delighted to meet you, Madame.

He kisses her full on the face. CECIL and NORFOLK watch with growing disapproval. ELIZABETH stares at ANJOU. He leans over and whispers into ELIZABETH's ear.

ANJOU: Vous êtes si belle. Je rêve du moment où nous serons nus ensemble, et je pourrai caresser votre peau nue et peut-etre la chatte. Non??
[You are so beautiful. I dream of the moment when we are naked together, and I can caress your naked skin and quinny. No??]

ELIZABETH is a little overwhelmed by his behaviour.

ELIZABETH: Please remove your hand. Perhaps, Your Grace, but I am very religious.

ANJOU: Ah – me too, me too! – Very religious!!

They walk passed an astonished court.

CUT TO: INT. NORFOLK'S CHAMBERS, WHITEHALL PALACE – DAY

NORFOLK walks forward towards the mirror dressed in his black, hooded Parliament robe. One of NORFOLK's MEN passes him his chain, which he puts on, staring at his reflection.
LETTICE moves towards him.

LETTICE: Must you leave?

NORFOLK places on his head his hat, which has also been passed to him.

NORFOLK: I would not miss this for the world. Today I shall watch the fall of that heretic girl.

Opposite top: *Behind the scenes*

Above and opposite: *The Duke of Anjou arrives with his entourage to meet Elizabeth*

The Duke of Anjou (Vincent Cassel)

CUT TO: INT. ELIZABETH'S BEDCHAMBER, WHITEHALL PALACE – DAY

ELIZABETH rehearses her speech for Parliament, stumbling over lines, stopping, starting again.

ELIZABETH: There is nothing about which I am more concerned than the people that I love, who love me.

I ask you to pass this Act of Uniformity. It is not for myself. It is for my people … My people.

There is a difference between a private person and the public self. Go hang yourselves, the lot of you. This Act of Uniformity … It is not for myself. It is for my people. They are my only care.

I have been placed here as your Sovereign … um … ah … No support. Stop it! This is for my people. My people are my care. My only care. Your grace. Where are the dogs today, my Lord?

I am willing to die a thousand times and there is nothing that I am more anxious about than the welfare of my people. My only care. They cannot . . . themselves. They cannot.

INT. GREAT HALL, PARLIAMENT – DAY

A noisy assembly. ELIZABETH sits upon the throne, flanked by CECIL and other COURTIERS. She is facing about two hundred MEMBERS OF PARLIAMENT, gathered in the great hall, most of them, even the BISHOPS, dressed in black.

NORFOLK *(sotto to SUSSEX)*: Where is Gardiner? Where are the others?

ELIZABETH: My Lords, if there is no uniformity of religious belief here, then there can only be fragmentation, dispute and quarrel! Surely it is better to have a single Church of England! A broad church, for all the people, with a common prayer book and common purpose …

There are loud mutterings of discontent.

ELIZABETH *(cont'd)*: I ask you to pass this Act of Uniformity – not for myself, but for my people, who are my only care!

SECOND BISHOP: Madam, by this act you force us to relinquish our allegiance to the Holy Father!

ELIZABETH: How could I force you, Your Grace? I am a woman. I have no desire to make windows into men's souls. I simply ask can any man in truth serve two masters and remain faithful to both?

Voices of dissent. Cries of "No, no, no!" NORFOLK and SUSSEX react.

NORFOLK: Like a lamb to slaughter.

THIRD BISHOP: This is heresy!

SECOND BISHOP: He is right. It is heresy indeed!

There is an explosion of sound, those agreeing, and those taking violent offence at the word, shouting: "Shame! Shame!"

ELIZABETH: No, your Grace. It is common sense – which is a most English virtue!

INT. CELLARS, PARLIAMENT – DAY

We see BISHOP GARDINER, with six other BISHOPS. They can hear the noise of laughter and argument above them. In anger and frustration GARDINER paces the cell.

FIRST BISHOP: This is Walsingham's doing, it is the devil's work …!

GARDINER: It will not serve her in any case. The bishops will pass no measure which severs them from Rome.
(beat) Come. Let us pray.

They continue praying in Latin. FIGURES in silhouette.

CUT TO: INT. GREAT HALL, PARLIAMENT – DAY

NORFOLK and SUSSEX are among the Lords.

FIRST BISHOP: Your Majesty would improve all these matters – if you would agree to marry!

ELIZABETH: Aye. But marry whom, your Grace? Will you give me some suggestion?

There is laughter.

ELIZABETH: For some say France, and others Spain, and some cannot abide foreigners at all, so I am not sure how best to please you, unless I married one of each!

More laughter. Now we see WALSINGHAM slip in, unobtrusively into the back of the room. But NORFOLK notices him and looks around.

LORD HAREWOOD: Now your Majesty does make fun of the sanctity of marriage.

ELIZABETH: I do not think you should lecture me on that, my Lord – since you yourself have been twice divorced, and are now upon your third wife!

Loud LAUGHTER at Harewood's expense. NORFOLK and SUSSEX exchange a worried look. Close on WALSINGHAM, who smiles at her bravery. There is laughter again, as many of the dissenting voices are stilled.

ELIZABETH: My Lords ... each of you must vote according to your conscience. But remember this: in your hands, upon this moment, lies the future happiness of my people, and the peace of this realm. Let that be upon your conscience also ...

CECIL: With your permission, Madam ... My Lords, the house will now divide.

INT. CELLARS – DAY

The seven BISHOPS, locked up, sitting it out. From a long way away, we hear the muffled sounds from the Great Hall in Parliament. The door is unlocked, opened.

GARDINER *(in fury)*: I would know on what authority you have kept us locked up here.

WALSINGHAM: Your Graces must forgive me – but you are now free to go.

GARDINER: I am sure this infernal work has not saved your bastard Queen.

WALSINGHAM's expression suddenly changes ... and for the first time we see the cold flicker of something indefinable behind his eyes. It is frightening.

WALSINGHAM: Her Majesty has won the argument.

GARDINER and the other BISHOPS stare at him.

GARDINER *(strangled)*: By what count?

WALSINGHAM: By five, Your Grace. By five.

The two men stare at each other with hatred. Then WALSINGHAM moves back up the stairs. GARDINER shouts after him.

GARDINER: You will be damned for this and I pray God that your wretched soul will burn in hell.

CUT TO: INT. CHAPEL, ST PETER'S, ROME – DAY

A sumptuous room, filled with icons, candles, statues and great works of art ...
  The POPE sits behind a desk, examining an official document. The CARDINAL carries a ladle of sealing wax to the POPE. He slowly pours the wax on to the document. The POPE, with a sudden firm gesture, stamps it upon the bottom of the Papal Bull.

INT. CHAMBER, ST PETER'S, ROME – DAY

A smaller but still sumptuous room. The CARDINAL enters the room, where ALVARO and BALLARD, the priest, await him.

CARDINAL: His Holiness has issued the Bull, Regnans in Excelsis …

ALVARO kisses his ring. The CARDINAL, carrying a small bundle of letters, crosses the room to BALLARD. As the CARDINAL moves to his desk, the camera moves in close on BALLARD.

CARDINAL: … It deprives Elizabeth, the pretended Queen of England, servant of wickedness, of her throne, and declares that henceforth her subjects are absolved of their allegiance to her.

ALVARO: Praise be to God.

CARDINAL: His Holiness also decrees that any man who should undertake her assassination will be welcomed by angels into the Kingdom of Heaven.

The CARDINAL holds out the letters to BALLARD.

CARDINAL: In good time, give these letters of blessing and hope to our friends in England.

EXT. RIVER THAMES – MIDSUMMER EVE

Lights gleam on the water – there is a pageant tonight. BOATS glide on the Thames, we hear the splash of oars and silken laughter and see white towers. A musicians' barge glides through the other boats. Music floats through the warm night air.

The Queen's barge, the stern formed into a gilded shell of red and gold, floats by.

EXT. ROYAL BARGE, RIVER THAMES – NIGHT

ELIZABETH lies back on cushions, like Cleopatra, with DUDLEY beside her, and only her LADIES in attendance. She laughs softly and sweetly with him as they feast on grapes and wine. She has never looked so beautiful as on this night, with pearls in her hair, her eyes shining …

As the barge floats beneath the bridge, PEOPLE call out to her and throw down flowers and small bags of spice, which scatter over the gleaming water. She laughs and waves back to them, intoxicated.

EXT. NORFOLK'S BARGE, RIVER THAMES – NIGHT

NORFOLK and SUSSEX look over at the Queen's barge, and see how ELIZABETH and DUDLEY laugh and sport themselves like young lovers.

EXT. ALVARO'S BARGE, RIVER THAMES – NIGHT

ALVARO also keeps close watch on ELIZABETH.

EXT. ROYAL BARGE, RIVER THAMES – NIGHT

We start on the water and the gleaming lights upon it. We hear DUDLEY's voice.
 Now we see ELIZABETH and DUDLEY as he sits beside her.

DUDLEY: My true love has my heart and I have hers. My heart in me keeps her and me in one. My heart in her, her thoughts and senses guide. She loves my heart, for once it was her own. I cherish hers because in me it bides. My true love has my heart, and I have hers.
(A beat) Marry me. Marry me.

At this moment fireworks light up the river. London is done up for carnival. CROWDS of people, many in masks, have come down to the river to watch the pageant. They carry torches and with much laughter crowd along the embankment. A wonderful fireworks display illuminates the river and its colourful barges.

EXT. ANJOU'S BARGE

ANJOU and DE FOIX also watch the royal barge, and perceive the same sight. The fireworks glow in the background.

ANJOU: La Reine semble être très intime avec Lord Robert – n'est ce pas?
 Avec moi elle joue la mégère, avec lui, l'amoureuse. Ne comprend-elle pas que sa vie même depends de mon consentement?
[The Queen seems most familiar with Lord Robert – does she not? With me she plays the shrew, with him the lover. Does she not know that her very life depends on my acceptance?]

DE FOIX: Monseigneur, vous devez comprendre qu'elle est une femme! … Elles disent une chose – mais veulent dire autre chose! Personne ne peut vraiment ouvrir leurs coeurs.
[Your Grace must understand that she is a woman! They say one thing – but mean another! No one can truly unlock their hearts.]

ANJOU giggles, behind his mask.

ANJOU: A moins qu'il ait une très grande clef! *(shouts)* Une très grande clef!
 [Unless he has a very large key!]

A Midsummer's Night Pageant

EXT. ROYAL BARGE, RIVER THAMES – NIGHT

Through the drapes we see ELIZABETH and DUDLEY flirting with one another.

ELIZABETH: On a night such as this, could any woman say no?

DUDLEY: On a night such as this could a Queen say no?

ELIZABETH: Does a Queen not sit under the same stars as any other woman?

He smiles at her, and sees ALVARO'S barge near by. There is mischief in his eyes as he jumps up and calls across to it.

DUDLEY: Monseigneur Alvaro! Monseigneur Alvaro!

ALVARO looks across from his barge.

DUDLEY: Tell me – as well as Ambassador, are you not also a bishop?

ALVARO: I am, my Lord.

ELIZABETH also looks out at ALVARO. He sees the suppressed excitement in both their eyes and knows he is being teased.

DUDLEY: Then you can marry us!

The look of shock on ALVARO's face makes them both burst into laughter.

ALVARO: Marry you?

ELIZABETH: Perhaps he does not know enough English to perform the ceremony!

ALVARO *(grimly)*: Alas, Madam, in this matter I can be of no help to you.

The boats drift apart. ELIZABETH and DUDLEY are still amused – though KAT watches them disapprovingly. From the darkness there is a thud. KAT looks up and screams as she sees the SOLDIER on guard topple through the curtains and fall across ELIZABETH.

KAT: Madam!

The drapes engulf ELIZABETH's face. DUDLEY turns from looking out to ALVARO. He pulls the SOLDIER off ELIZABETH, revealing a dart lodged in his chest. DUDLEY moves swiftly to her, pulling the drape from around her.

DUDLEY *(calling out)*: The Queen! Look to the Queen!

Suddenly another dart pins ELIZABETH down.

CUT TO: EXT. NORFOLK'S BARGE, RIVER THAMES – NIGHT

NORFOLK turns and exchanges a significant glance with SUSSEX, though his features remain unmoved.

CUT TO: EXT. ANJOU'S BARGE, RIVER THAMES – NIGHT

DE FOIX's and ANJOU's attention is caught.

INT. PRIVY CHAMBER CORRIDORS, WHITEHALL PALACE – NIGHT

There is turmoil inside the palace, as ELIZABETH, her dress still soaked with blood, is hurried towards the Privy Chambers, under heavy guard, and escorted by CECIL.

KAT *(V.O.)*: Get the bedchamber ready, Isabel! Go!

WALSINGHAM appears as they cross into the Privy Chamber.

CECIL: I only pray that her Majesty be safely delivered from this present danger.

CECIL follows on after the entourage. WALSINGHAM watches for a moment, gives last instructions to his man, leaves. As he does so, DUDLEY enters the Privy Chamber. As ELIZABETH nears the bedchamber, two of her LADIES run to her. KAT is still anxiously protecting her Queen.

ELIZABETH: I am perfectly well. Please do not fuss.

CECIL, following on, instructs an OFFICER of the Guard. DUDLEY walks towards them.

CECIL: No one is to enter.

The OFFICER turns to DUDLEY.

OFFICER: Sorry, my Lord.

CECIL: No one.

DUDLEY stares at CECIL, before turning away.

INT. ELIZABETH'S BEDCHAMBER, WHITEHALL PALACE – NIGHT

Behind a screen, KAT and ISABEL begin to strip off ELIZABETH's bloody dress. Blood is sponged from her skin. CECIL remains on the other side of the screen.

CECIL: Madam, if you would only heed my advice.

ELIZABETH: I have narrowly escaped with my life, Sir. I cannot now discuss marriage.

CECIL *(V.O.)*: Forgive me, Madam, the one cannot be separated from the other! Have I not told you?

ELIZABETH *(sharp)*: Yes! And I am sick of it.

CUT TO: INT. CORRIDORS, WHITEHALL PALACE – NIGHT

ALVARO speaks to DUDLEY in the shadows of a corridor.

ALVARO: I see it is true that the Queen favours you above all others – but you have many enemies here. Is it not so?

DUDLEY: That is no concern of yours.

ALVARO: It may be. If you would be prepared, in secret, to renounce heresy and embrace the true faith, then you might find many new and powerful friends – and keep your Queen.

DUDLEY: You are most mistaken, Monseigneur, if you think I might so easily be persuaded to act against my conscience – and my love.

DUDLEY moves away. ALVARO calls to him.

ALVARO: Ah, my Lord – what will a man not do ... for love?

DUDLEY does not reply, but stares at him. The expression on ALVARO's face changes. WALSINGHAM passes the place where ALVARO and DUDLEY are huddled in the shadows. He appears not to notice them and passes on his way. DUDLEY leaves.

CUT TO: INT. ELIZABETH'S BEDCHAMBER, WHITEHALL PALACE – NIGHT

KAT and ISABEL place a fresh robe around ELIZABETH. She comes out from behind the screen.

ELIZABETH: This entire conversation is ill timed. My patience is not infinite.

ELIZABETH stops short, surprised to see DE FOIX standing beside CECIL. He bows.

DE FOIX: It is a great joy to see your Majesty is not hurt. It was a terrible affair!

ELIZABETH does not respond, but stares at them.

CECIL: The Duke would still know the answer to his suit.

ELIZABETH *(composing herself)*: You may tell the Duke that he will have his answer shortly.

CECIL: But Madam, the point is pressing!

ELIZABETH *(a flash of irritation)*: The Duke cannot love me so much, if he demands my answer so precipitously!

DE FOIX smiles a little.

DE FOIX: Perhaps her Majesty will not answer, because her heart is already set upon another.

ELIZABETH: Do not presume, Monsieur, to know the secrets of my heart! Monsieur De Foix may leave.

She turns her back on them. DE FOIX is abashed, turns and leaves.

CECIL: S'il vous plaît, Excellence. Je m'excuse.

CECIL turns to ELIZABETH. KAT and ISABEL make up her bed.

CECIL *(cont'd)*: Secrets, Madam. You have no secrets. The world knows that Lord Robert visits your chambers at night and that you fornicate with him. It is even said that you already carry his child.

ELIZABETH steels herself.

ELIZABETH: Yes, Sir William, I live my life is the open, and I am always surrounded by people ...

ELIZABETH glares at KAT angrily.

ELIZABETH *(cont'd)*: ... but I do not understand how so bad a judgement has been formed of me.

CECIL: Madam! You cannot marry Lord Robert! ... He is already married!

CUT TO: INT. WALSINGHAM'S CHAMBER, WHITEHALL PALACE – NIGHT

Dark and shadowy ... candles flicker. There are books everywhere. WALSINGHAM paces the room – ELYOT watching him.

ELYOT: I do not understand, sir.

WALSINGHAM: Learn to ponder upon complexities. For what appears simple, may not be so. When noone sees – so the mind must seek.

ELYOT: To whose advantage was this? De Foix?

WALSINGHAM: No. Not with Anjou in play.

ELYOT: Then some madman.

WALSINGHAM: There is always madness. But this was devised. There is reason behind it.

ELYOT: Then Alvaro – for he has most cause.

A beat. WALSINGHAM shakes his head.

WALSINGHAM: Yes, yes, yes. But he was present. He is more subtle than that.

ELYOT: Would Norfolk? He is not so subtle ...

WALSINGHAM: Indeed.

ELYOT *(cont'd)*: ... And has even more cause. So then maybe he's not in league with the Spanish.

WALSINGHAM smiles a little.

WALSINGHAM: The Duke has some other game. I must find the way he plays.

CUT TO: EXT. CUMNOR HALL, OXFORDSHIRE – DAY

A peaceful, secluded old manor. We see some hens and ducks scratching around in the yard, a tethered goat. We hear the music of a virginal.

INT. GALLERY, CUMNOR HALL, OXFORDSHIRE

At the far end, a young woman is playing the virginal. AMY RONSART, Dudley's wife, is a pretty and fresh-faced country girl. She continues to play for a few moments, then hears the creak of the floorboards, and looks up to see two MEN walking towards her. They neither bow nor check. She stares at them.

AMY: Where are my servants? What is it? Did Lord Robert send you here?

She cries as the MEN take hold of her. Camera looking down a staircase. Sounds of scuffles and screams. AMY's body comes rolling into frame and falls farther down the stairs, her dead face coming awkwardly to rest as the men's boots step over it.

INT. COURT, WHITEHALL PALACE – DAY

The court is seething with rumour. NORFOLK and SUSSEX stand amid their MEN, dressed in yellow. DUDLEY crosses the court. Silence.

NORFOLK *(calls out)*: Lord Robert! We are amazed that you show your face at court!

DUDLEY: Why amazed, your Grace?

SUSSEX: Because you are a murderer!

DUDLEY looks at SUSSEX with contempt.

DUDLEY: Does the dog speak for his master?

SUSSEX: Poor, sad, buxom, country Amy! Who else can we blame?

DUDLEY: You had cause enough, Your Grace! You are not so innocent!

NORFOLK: I would not wet my finger on such a wench ... But you would whore with anyone!

A beat. They see that ELIZABETH has appeared, with CECIL and her LADIES. She looks at them – then moves across the court. As she passes through the crowd she is conscious of people staring at her.

CECIL: We will, gentlemen, summon council.

NORFOLK and SUSSEX follow CECIL out. DUDLEY remains isolated.

INT. COURT, WHITEHALL PALACE – NIGHT

ELIZABETH is in the centre of the room, where a PANTOMIME is in full swing. MEN dressed as Spanish galleons "float" in a makeshift sea and are buffeted and attacked by other MEN dressed as English cutters. There is laughter from the French and English camps. The Spanish camp is sombre.

ELIZABETH watches this accompanied by CECIL and DE FOIX with KAT in attendance. Across the room ALVARO sits beside NORFOLK and SUSSEX.

ALVARO: It is not enough that English pirates attack and rob our ships, but we are to be made fools of in this court!

NORFOLK looks at him.

ALVARO: The King, my master, has become impatient for Your Grace to act. If you will not … then others may.

NORFOLK: You must reassure his Majesty that the time for action is close at hand. But he must not act precipitously.

ALVARO looks at him shrewdly.

ALVARO: His Majesty has also heard a rumour …

NORFOLK: The world is filled with rumours, Monseigneur!

ALVARO: … That Your Grace has made contact with the French, and Mary of Scots, to promote your ambitions! Even that you mean to marry her!

NORFOLK: Do you suppose me an idiot?! Your master is the most powerful man in the world. I would not cross him for my life … nor waste it on that French whore!

ALVARO nods – but his eyes remain suspicious.

Cut to: WALSINGHAM, who silently enters the room, watching. DUDLEY passes him but stops by the LADIES-IN-WAITING seated together at a table. He flirts briefly with the ravishing ISABEL.

ELIZABETH leans back and turns to DE FOIX, who is at her side.

ELIZABETH: Will the Duke not come to dance?

DE FOIX: Madam, his Grace is unfortunately indisposed. He has some pains – of the stomach.

ELIZABETH: I am very sorry for it. We wished to give him this ring, as a token of our love.

She slips the ring from her finger, offers it to him – then withdraws it.

ELIZABETH: No. I shall give it to the Duke myself.

She starts to move away. CECIL is about to follow, but she holds a hand out to stop him.

ELIZABETH: Sir William …

DE FOIX blanches.

DE FOIX: Madam … I should not …

DE FOIX has no choice. He bows to CECIL and follows her out.

INT. ANJOU'S CHAMBERS, WHITEHALL PALACE – NIGHT

In a candlelit room, a table is laden with sumptuous food. A YOUNG WOMAN, half naked, is caressed by a YOUNG MAN.

ELIZABETH appears through the sheer drapes, followed by KAT and DE FOIX. The couple scramble to cover themselves.

In another room, ELIZABETH parts the drapes. There are YOUNG MEN and WOMEN of the court lounging voluptuously around the room, some in a state of undress. When they see the Queen they scramble to their feet, trying to adjust their clothing, bowing, faces white with fear. ELIZABETH, without a word, moves past them – still hearing high-pitched laughter.

Another room is seen through a gauze hanging. More YOUNG MEN, half-naked, caressing sensually a single WOMAN in a glittering dress, like a Queen.

ANJOU: What? You stare, Madam? Why? Do you see something strange, perhaps?

ELIZABETH: You are wearing a dress, Your Grace!

ANJOU: Yes, yes, I am wearing a dress, like my mother. I only dress like this when I am alone with friends. Always in private! J'aime la soie Francaise!
[I love French silk!]
It is not important.

ELIZABETH: Your Grace, although my affection for you is undiminished, I have after an agonizing struggle, determined to sacrifice my own happiness for the welfare of my people.

ELIZABETH moves away. DE FOIX hurries after her.

DE FOIX: Madame! I will explain …

ELIZABETH: Ce n'est pas la peine, Excellence. Je comprends tout.
[There is no need, Excellency. I understand everything.]

DE FOIX watches ELIZABETH and KAT walk away. ANJOU ushers him away after them. ANJOU shouts at the MUSICIANS.

ANJOU: Jouez! Jouez!

The Duke of Anjou dressed as a woman

CUT TO: INT. COURT, WHITEHALL PALACE – NIGHT

ELIZABETH and KAT return to the court. The tension is palpable ... everyone is watching her. She walks over to CECIL and sits next to him.

CECIL: Madam ... is the Duke ... ?

ELIZABETH: Sir William! Speak to me no more of marriage!

CECIL notices DE FOIX enter the court. They exchange looks. ELIZABETH suddenly begins to laugh ... The tension is broken. She calls out to DUDLEY as he appears through an archway, near to the LADIES-IN-WAITING.

ELIZABETH: Lord Robert.

DUDLEY: Your Majesty.

ELIZABETH: Will you dance?

DUDLEY: If it please you.

ELIZABETH stands and crosses to face him. She looks over at the MUSICIANS.

ELIZABETH: Play a volta!

The MUSICIANS strike up. CECIL joins DE FOIX. ELIZABETH and DUDLEY begin to dance, watched by SUSSEX, NORFOLK, ALVARO, WALSINGHAM ... the whole court.

DUDLEY: You must not believe what they tell you. They are jealous and envious ... because I owe nothing to them, and everything to you.

ELIZABETH *(interrupting)*: Did you love her?

There is a flicker of panic in his eyes.

DUDLEY: No, I love you. I have always loved you ...

ELIZABETH looks at him. He throws her into the air and catches her.

DUDLEY *(cont'd)*: I was afraid of losing you because I was not free ...

She still looks at him. DUDLEY panics. He grips her. The whole court has become aware of the tension.

DUDLEY *(cont'd)*: For God's sake, you are still my Elizabeth!

Thomas Elyot (Kenny Doughty) is confronted by John Ballard (Daniel Craig)

He throws her again – but this time fails to catches her properly, and she stumbles awkwardly … There is a communal gasp from the watching COURTIERS … She faces him and there is a dangerous look in her eyes.

ELIZABETH: I am not your Elizabeth! I am no man's Elizabeth! And if you think to rule here, you are mistaken …

ELIZABETH walks away towards the entrance, then turns back.

ELIZABETH *(cont'd)*: I will have one mistress here, and no master!

She stares at him, then sweeps away. WALSINGHAM

follows. DUDLEY exchanges looks with ALVARO and then leaves.

EXT. WHITEHALL PALACE – NIGHT

DE FOIX walks quickly with a humiliated ANJOU to their carriage, accompanied by another MAN, whose face we do not see. ANJOU gesticulates to both men. The carriage drives away into the night. DE FOIX and the other MAN walk towards camera, and we see it is WALSINGHAM.

EXT. COAST OF ENGLAND – DAWN

A misty dawn. A group of MEN in Norfolk's colours

leading a couple of riderless horses ride along a beach below a castle. Above on the rocks stands NORFOLK and ALVARO accompanied by ELYOT, looking out to sea.

Out at sea a small boat can be seen approaching. The boat arrives on shore and BALLARD and another PRIEST jump out. Waiting to greet them is NORFOLK and ALVARO. ELYOT stands a little apart. BALLARD kisses NORFOLK's ring.

BALLARD: Your Grace ...
(to ALVARO) Monseigneur ...

He moves towards ELYOT and smiles.

BALLARD *(to ELYOT):* ... Thomas Elyot. You serve your master well, Elyot.

A flicker of unease crosses ELYOT's face.

ELYOT: As well as I can, in truth.

BALLARD: I mean your real master.
NORFOLK looks puzzled.

NORFOLK: What's this? What master?

BALLARD: Walsingham.

ELYOT: The priest is mistaken. I am Your Grace's servant as God is my witness.
A beat. BALLARD lunges forward suddenly and grabs ELYOT by the neck. He drags him to the water's edge.

BALLARD: Your God doesn't hear you – heretic!

He thrusts ELYOT's head underwater, and violently hits him with a stone. NORFOLK watches from the beach.
BALLARD makes his way back towards the others. ELYOT's lifeless body lies face downwards in a pool of water. NORFOLK's MEN wipe the frame with their horses.

CUT TO: INT. NORFOLK'S CHAMBERS, WHITEHALL PALACE – DAY

Through a half-open doorway, we see BALLARD. He bows then walks out through the door revealing ALVARO. After a pause, ALVARO follows. As he leaves, NORFOLK is revealed seated at a table, watching. LETTICE closes the door.

CUT TO: INT. ELIZABETH'S BEDCHAMBER, WHITEHALL PALACE

ISABEL picks up one of ELIZABETH's dresses, crosses to the mirror, and looks up at herself. As she replaces the dress she finds an even more beautiful one. We see the reflection of ISABEL in a mirror holding this dress up to her.

INT. COURT, WHITEHALL PALACE – NIGHT

ISABEL slips through the shadows. Looking carefully, almost furtively around, she goes quickly down some stairs, across a dark courtyard, climbs another short set of stairs to a door, pauses and then slips inside.

INT. ROOM, COURT, WHITEHALL PALACE – NIGHT

ISABEL and a MAN are making love in the shadows against a wall. We cannot see who he is. ISABEL is wearing the exquisite dress.

ISABEL *(seductive):* Look! I am Queen!

They continue to make love against the wall.

ISABEL: Say you are mine ...

He continues, aggressively, urgently, to taking his pleasure with her.

ISABEL *(continuing her plea):* Say you are mine ...

MAN: Say you are my Elizabeth.

ISABEL: I am your Queen.

He is oblivious, his lovemaking frantic. ISABEL writhes and moans beneath him. We think she is in the full throes of passion, but then suddenly it is clear that she is in deep distress as she tries to push him away from her and her moans become cries of pain. She is pulling at the dress, scratching and clawing at her skin.
We pull back to reveal that her lover is DUDLEY.
ISABEL screams and screams again, pulling at her dress, rolling on the floor. DUDLEY, afraid of being caught, tries to put his hand over her mouth to stop her but she bites his hand, and screams again ...

Isabel Knollys (Kelly MacDonald)

DUDLEY, filled now with panic, runs out of the room and disappears. ISABEL slides down the wall, on to the floor, screaming, clawing at herself...

CUT TO: INT. COURT, WHITEHALL PALACE – NIGHT

ELIZABETH walks out through the pillars, into the court. No one is there. The soldiers who normally guard the doors are gone. She is alone ... in the eerie quiet.

ELIZABETH (confused): Kat? ... Kat Ashley? Kat?

She hurries forward, alarmed, looking for somebody. And then hears footsteps approaching ... quickening. A cloaked and hooded figure, BALLARD, is coming towards her.

ELIZABETH (becoming alarmed): Walsingham? (She looks over her shoulder.) Who are you ... ? You will declare yourself to me ...

The hooded FIGURE reaches into the folds of his clothes. Suddenly KAT appears.

KAT: Madam!

A GUARD is in her wake.

ELIZABETH: Where is everybody ... ? Where were you ... ?

KAT (hysterical): Come quickly, something has happened, you must come with me.

As ELIZABETH looks back, the hooded FIGURE has gone. She follows KAT. Close on BALLARD, hurrying off.

INT. CORRIDOR, COURT, WHITEHALL PALACE – NIGHT

ELIZABETH and KAT run into the corridor. ELIZABETH looks down upon the still form of ISABEL, her skin a mass of flayed red and bloody tissue. The dress is ripped and torn, spotted with blood. CECIL quickly moves to ELIZABETH.

CECIL: No, Madam, no! The dress was poisoned.

ELIZABETH stares, alarm dawning in her face.

ELIZABETH: That dress was a gift ... for me.

CECIL: French silk!

CUT TO: EXT. LEITH CASTLE – NIGHT

One word appear on the screen: SCOTLAND.
The castle sits, grim and huge, atop a rock, the walls sheer and impregnable, the flag of MARY OF GUISE flying.

EXT. COURTYARD, LEITH CASTLE – NIGHT

FRENCH TROOPS stand around the courtyard as a covered wagon drives in. We see PEOPLE step out, walking into the doorway of the Castle. We recognise one of them, from behind, as WALSINGHAM.

INT. PRIVATE DINING ROOM, LEITH CASTLE – NIGHT

We see MARY OF GUISE, ANJOU, two FRENCH COURTIERS, and then WALSINGHAM. MARY OF GUISE is looking at him carefully.

MARY OF GUISE: Sir Francis, you and I … we must be honest with each other, non?

She is interrupted by violent sneezing. The source is

ANJOU, who has a heavy head cold; his face is plunged into the steam from a bowl of hot water and spices, his head covered with a cloth. He pulls the cloth off to reveal himself. He impatiently dismisses the MAID, who tries to serve him, then covers his head with the cloth again.

MARY OF GUISE *(cont'd)*: Your Queen is weak – she has no army, no friends … Comment vous dites çà déjà – enemies?

        [How do you say?]

WALSINGHAM: Enemies.

MARY OF GUISE *(cont'd)*: What terms can she propose?

ANJOU peeps out from under his cloth – watching them.

WALSINGHAM: Madam, her Majesty was, I believe, too hasty in rejecting the Duke's proposal of marriage.

ANJOU emerges from under the cloth and bangs his fist on the table.

ANJOU: But how can I marry such a woman? She is frigid! They say she is really a man!

MARY OF GUISE looks at him severely.

MARY OF GUISE *(to ANJOU)*: Allez vous coucher! Et laissez-moi arranger tout çà.
[Go to bed! Leave me to arrange this.]

ANJOU: Non, ma tante.
[No, aunt.]

MARY OF GUISE: Non! Ne me forcez pas à venir vous chercher.
[Don't force me to make you.]

(to WALSINGHAM) You must forgive my nephew. He speaks when he should not.

ANJOU looks fierce for a moment, then nods meekly, kisses his aunt on the mouth and stares tauntingly at WALSINGHAM. He calls to the others to leave, then tosses the remains of his chicken bone towards WALSINGHAM and withdraws. MARY signals them to leave. They do so.

MARY OF GUISE *(to ANJOU)*: Et ne faites pas l'enfant Henri!
[And don't fool around, Henri!]

MARY leans close towards WALSINGHAM.

MARY OF GUISE *(to WALSINGHAM)*: I hear you are a wise man, Sir Francis, and a creature of the world … Like me!

She laughs. WALSINGHAM looks back at her. At this moment a MAID interrupts, offering to refill their cups. MARY gestures her away.

WALSINGHAM: I have no illusions. I know it is only a matter of time before my Queen is overthrown. Her Majesty rules with the heart – not with the head.

MARY OF GUISE nods.

MARY OF GUISE: I understand it is hard for a woman to forget her heart …

(Smiles) But … what of you … Walsingham?

WALSINGHAM: A wise man would be careful not to put himself in the way of harm.

MARY OF GUISE: And how would a wise man do that?

WALSINGHAM: He would, as I said, change his allegiance.

MARY OF GUISE: Allegiance.

WALSINGHAM: There are but two choices: he would – comment dire çà? –
[How do you say?]
… get into bed with either Spain … or France …

MARY OF GUISE *(laughs)*: And whose bed would you prefer?

The MAID places a bowl of fruit on the table – breaking them apart – and MARY sits back, looking at WALSINGHAM.

CUT TO: INT. STAIRCASE, LEITH CASTLE – NIGHT

A MAID climbs up a dark, winding back staircase. She carries a tray. The candlelight on the tray lights her face, and a decanter of wine beside the candles.

INT. MARY OF GUISE'S BEDCHAMBER, LEITH CASTLE – NIGHT

The candle flickers. The MAID opens the door to Mary's bedchamber and enters. WALSINGHAM leads MARY across the room. He undos her chemise, which falls to the ground. Through a billowing curtain and without a word we see WALSINGHAM touch her face and body.

WALSINGHAM: Vous êtes très belle!
[You are very beautiful!]

MARY OF GUISE: You lie. But it is good to hear.

MARY smiles at him.

INT. ELIZABETH'S BEDCHAMBER, WHITEHALL PALACE – DAY

ELIZABETH sits on her throne. A SCRIBE holds some papers, which she is signing. Her LADIES sit at her feet. DUDLEY enters.

DUDLEY: Your Majesty. May I speak with you in private?

ELIZABETH *(without looking at him)*: Speak!

DUDLEY: You are in the greatest danger. You must believe me!

She looks at him but does not respond.

DUDLEY: But you have a friend, someone who can guarantee your safety, and your throne.

She stares at him.

ELIZABETH: A friend?

DUDLEY: The King of Spain …

DUDLEY glances at the LADIES-IN-WAITING. ELIZABETH gestures them away.

ELIZABETH: Leave us.

The LADIES scatter – ELIZABETH stands and crosses to DUDLEY.

ELIZABETH: How would he guarantee it?

DUDLEY: He would marry you …
(Quickly) Only to make an alliance! Nothing more. He would not expect to … He would live in Spain …

ELIZABETH: Why do you do this, Robert?

DUDLEY: Because I love you – and though you will not see me, I am the only one who would care for you.

ELIZABETH: You love me so much you would have me be your whore?

She turns away from him, and up to her throne.

DUDLEY *(shouts)*: For God's sake – I ask you to do this for us. I ask you to save some part of us.

She looks back.

ELIZABETH: Lord Robert. You may make whores of my ladies – but you will not make one of me!

DUDLEY *(after a beat)*: Your Majesty.

DUDLEY bows and exits.

EXT. LEITH CASTLE – DAWN

Dawn breaks over the castle battlements.

INT. MARY OF GUISE'S BEDCHAMBER, LEITH CASTLE – DAWN

MARY OF GUISE lies dead in bed. The MAID and a few COURTIERS watch in silence as ANJOU lies over her body in a paroxysm of grief, kissing her cold lips, screaming out:

ANJOU: C'est une sorcière et ses serviteurs, des diables! Des diables! Sortez! Sortez! Sortez!
[She is a witch – and all her servants, devils! Devils! Get out! Get out! Get out!]

They slowly begin to move out of the room.

INT. ELIZABETH'S PRIVY CHAMBERS, WHITEHALL PALACE – DAY

We see ELIZABETH behind gauze drapes. She is eating. Behind her is KAT and out in the main chambers stands CECIL, with WALSINGHAM near by watching.

ELIZABETH *(eating)*: Of course I shall deny it.

CECIL: But your Majesty must publicly disassociate yourself from this most bloody act!

ELIZABETH: I never ordered it.

CECIL: Of course, Madam, of course. You must also make conciliatory gestures towards the Spanish. Your dependence upon their good will is even greater than ever. I really must insist that …

ELIZABETH: The word must is not used to princes!

He blanches. ELIZABETH moves out from the drapes to her throne – KAT follows.

ELIZABETH *(cont'd):* I have followed your advice in all the affairs of my kingdom, but your policies would make England nothing but either part of France or of Spain!
(A beat) From this moment, I am going to follow my own opinion and see if I do any better.

CECIL is confused.

CECIL: Madam, forgive me – you are only a woman!

ELIZABETH: I may be a woman, Sir William – but if I choose, I have the heart of a man. You forget, sir, I am my father's daughter. I am not afraid of anything!

There is a pause. CECIL is suddenly contrite.

CECIL: I regret that I have caused your Majesty such offence – though God knows all my advice has only been to secure your Majesty's throne.

A beat. ELIZABETH smiles.

ELIZABETH: I am grateful for it. I have decided to create you Lord Burghley, so you may enjoy your retirement in greater ease.

CECIL looks at her.

CECIL: Madam …

ELIZABETH *(curtly):* That will be all, Lord Burghley.

She offers her hand, and CECIL kisses it. CECIL backs away from her and as he turns he finds WALSINGHAM uncomfortably close. He looks straight at WALSINGHAM and understands. He leaves.

ELIZABETH crosses to sit at the long table. She opens her drawing book and begins painting a flower in a vase, seemingly involved in copying it. WALSINGHAM moves closer to her.

WALSINGHAM: Madam, if I may … A prince should never flinch from being blamed for acts of ruthlessness which are necessary for safeguarding the state, and their own person. You must take these things so much to heart that you do not fear to strike even the very nearest that you have, if they be implicated.

A beat. He stares at her.

WALSINGHAM *(cont'd)*: It has been made known to me there is a priest abroad in the land, carrying letters from Rome to those who will not flinch and do mean to harm you.

A beat. ELIZABETH continues with her painting. WALSINGHAM goes out.

INT. COURT, WHITEHALL PALACE – NIGHT

NORFOLK enters the court, with a large entourage, and his two great hunting dogs behind him. He has all the manner and swagger of a King.

COURTIERS crowd around him, bowing – not only the Catholics like SUSSEX and ARUNDEL, but also Protestants like DERBY and THROCKMORTON. NORFOLK passes DUDLEY, who acknowledges him.

ELIZABETH enters with KAT and the other LADIES. Though people still bow to her she cannot help but notice how many of them wear yellow – Norfolk's colour. She crosses over to him, in full view of everyone.

ELIZABETH: Your Grace.

NORFOLK *(bowing, ironic)*: Majesty.

ELIZABETH: I would walk with you a little, in private.

ELIZABETH and NORFOLK walk out, followed by her Ladies-in-Waiting. The whole court observes.

CUT TO: INT. LADY CHAPEL, WHITEHALL PALACE – DAY

ELIZABETH kneels by an altar. She gestures to NORFOLK to join her.

ELIZABETH: Your Grace?

NORFOLK takes his place and kneels beside her.

ELIZABETH (*cont'd*): We have heard that pirates who claim to be English are attacking Spanish ships, and robbing them. It is without our permission – but I fear the Spanish will take it as just cause to retaliate against us. I know you have great influence with the Spanish. By your good grace, I would hope to be conciliated with them.

She stops, looks at him, and puts her hand upon his. She looks young and vulnerable.

ELIZABETH (*cont'd. Almost pleadingly*)**:** Will you do it – for my sake?

NORFOLK, almost visibly bloated by arrogance, looks back at her.

NORFOLK: Aye, Madam. I will – for your sake … and for England's.

NORFOLK leaves. ELIZABETH is alone with her thoughts.

CUT TO: EXT. ROWING BOAT – NIGHT

We are close on the water, as a pair of oars dip into the swell.
 In the small rowing boat, beside the OARSMAN, are two FIGURES, muffled in black: WALSINGHAM and ELIZABETH. Ahead of them, across the sound, the lights of a great ship gleam dimly.

INT. SHIP'S OAK-LINED STATE ROOM – NIGHT

ELIZABETH sits at a table, surrounded by the weathered faces of twelve SEA CAPTAINS.

ELIZABETH: My good Captains, you are men of the sea, honest and direct. So let me be honest and direct with you. You have no licence from me to steal from Spanish ships.

Now there are murmurs of protest.

ELIZABETH: I said I could not give you licence! I did not say you should not do it!

She smiles. They realise what she has said.

FIRST CAPTAIN: You would not call it … piracy?

ELIZABETH: On the contrary. I should call it … good enterprise.

SECOND CAPTAIN: And whatever we should happen to catch?

ELIZABETH: In future, what you … catch shall be divided. One quarter shall be yours, but with the rest we shall begin to build a fleet that shall make England proud again, and master of her fate!

WALSINGHAM watches with approval, standing among the men. ELIZABETH smiles, and rises to her feet.

ELIZABETH: I bid you good fishing, my brave Captains!

ELIZABETH raises her glass and they all stand and shout "Good fishing, your Majesty!"

CUT TO: INT. ARUNDEL'S HOUSE – NIGHT

The sound of KNOCKING. SERVANTS scurry, panic-stricken, through corridors.
    SOLDIERS burst in and fan out through the house. WALSINGHAM enters and goes directly to the NURSE-MAID who stands at the bottom of the stairs, frightened amid the chaos, protecting the CHILDREN. He picks up the little GIRL.

WALSINGHAM: Where is Lord Arundel?

NURSEMAID: He is not here.

Cut to: SOLDIERS scattered, searching throughout the house.

CUT TO: INT. DINING ROOM

WALSINGHAM puts down the little GIRL. He turns to the BOY.

WALSINGHAM: Do you know where your father is?

The BOY does not answer, but WALSINGHAM notices as he glances toward a panel on the wall.

WALSINGHAM signals to a GUARD, who moves towards the wall and taps the panels. WALSINGHAM joins him and discovers a panel that slides down to reveal a handle. The GUARD turns it and inside is a small hidden chapel; candles flicker, and there are icons and images of the Virgin Mary everywhere.

ARUNDEL and his WIFE are taking mass at a small altar, led by BALLARD. They react, startled.

INT. TORTURE CHAMBER, TOWER OF LONDON – NIGHT

BALLARD is suspended by chains from the ceiling, his feet not quite touching the floor, the sinews in his arms and the veins upon his neck bulging frighteningly. He is in agony, his body and face black with bruises. His head is bent backwards, his face at a strange angle. WALSINGHAM's face appears adjacent to it, very close.

WALSINGHAM: You were carrying letters … from the Pope … To whom were you told to give them?

No response. WALSINGHAM nods to the TORTURER, who puts a torch to BALLARD's skin. He cries out. The

TORTURER moves away.

WALSINGHAM: Tell me, what is your God to you? Where is He now? Has He not abandoned you?

BALLARD shakes his head violently.

WALSINGHAM *(cont'd)***:** Or is He such a worldly God that He must play at politics – and the filth of conspiracy!? Is He not divine? Tell me the truth – as if you were face to face with Him now!

WALSINGHAM signals again to the TORTURER, who now takes the hook and digs downwards with the hook.

WALSINGHAM: I am a patient man, Father.

The TORTURER digs downwards with the knife. There is a spurt of blood.

BALLARD: Pace mihi, Domine Jesu …

INT. ELIZABETH'S PRIVY CHAMBERS, WHITEHALL PALACE – NIGHT

ELIZABETH is alone with WALSINGHAM, examining the Pope's letters.

WALSINGHAM: Sussex … Gardiner … Arundel … and … Lord Robert Dudley, Earl of Leicester.

ELIZABETH tries to contain her pain.

ELIZABETH: A man will confess to anything under torture.

He produces an official-looking document.

WALSINGHAM *(cont'd)*: But Madam, this document was also found among the priest's possessions.

WALSINGHAM: From his Holiness the Pope to his Grace, The Duke of Norfolk, "To legitimize your claim to the throne of England, his Holiness proposes that you should take as your bride Mary, Queen of Scots, cousin to Elizabeth …

ELIZABETH: … the illegitimate and heretical … whore who now … sits upon the throne.

WALSINGHAM: All Norfolk need do is sign this paper and the treason will have been committed.

ELIZABETH *(looks up at him)*: Then – let him sign it! And let it be done.

CUT TO: INT. NORFOLK'S CHAMBERS, WHITEHALL PALACE – NIGHT

NORFOLK sits at his table, the Pope's letter in front of him. LETTICE leans against the bedpost.

NORFOLK *(to LETTICE)*: In the future, when England is safe again, and faithful, they will thank me for this act and forget the manner of it. Is it not true?

LETTICE joins him at the table and nods, almost imperceptibly. NORFOLK dips the quill into the ink and signs the letter with a firm hand. He rolls the letter up and hands it to LETTICE.

NORFOLK: Deliver this most carefully.

LETTICE takes the letter and leaves the chamber. NORFOLK signals one of his MEN forward.

NORFOLK: Go at once to our estates. We shall need 50,000 armed men in the field, as soon as my marriage is … consummated.

NORFOLK's MAN bows and leaves. NORFOLK is alone. He picks up his quill once again, and begins to write hurriedly.

CUT TO: INT. LADY CHAPEL, WHITEHALL PALACE – NIGHT

ELIZABETH listens to a William Byrd mass. A CHOIR of young boys (not in shot) sing the high and complex, spiritual, ethereal music. Tears roll down her cheeks as she prays, alone.

CUT TO: INT. ARMOURY – NIGHT

WALSINGHAM watches the handing out of swords and pikes to a large group of his men. One of the men presents him with a sword.

WALSINGHAM: The time is ripe. So, as you will, take them into your cold hands.

CUT TO: INT. ARUNDEL'S HOUSE – NIGHT

We see the CHILDREN asleep on the bed in their mother's lap. ARUNDEL moves from the fireplace to the bed, places a blanket over the little GIRL and tucks her up.

CUT TO: INT. LAVATORIES – NIGHT

SUSSEX sits on the lavatory in the stench-filled room. He begins to relieve himself ...

CUT TO: INT. NORFOLK'S BEDCHAMBER, WHITE-HALL PALACE – NIGHT

Through the black drapes we see NORFOLK and LETTICE making love on his bed.

CUT TO: INT. GARDINER CELL, MONASTIC BUILDING – NIGHT

Stripped to the waist, BISHOP GARDINER flays himself, ripping the skin from his back ... at the same time chanting a prayer.

GARDINER: Confiteor Deo omnipotenti, beatae Mariae semper Virgini, beato Michaeli Archangelo, beato Ioanni Baptistae, sanctis Apostolis Petro et Paulo, omnibus Sanctis, et vobis, fratres (et tibi pater), quia peccavi nimis cogitatione, verbo et opere: mea culpa, mea culpa, mea maxima culpa. Ideo precor

beatam Mariam semper Virginem, beatum Michaelem Archangelem, beatum Ioannem Baptistam, sanctos Apostolos Petrum et Paulum, omnes Sanctos, et vos, fratres (et te, pater), orare pro me ad Dominum Deum nostrum. Amen.

[I confess to almighty God, to blessed Mary ever Virgin, to blessed Michael the archangel, to blessed John the Baptist, to the holy apostles Peter and Paul, to all the saints, and to you my brothers and sisters (and to thee, father) that I have sinned exceedingly in thought, word, and deed, through my fault, through my fault, through my most grievous fault. Therefore, I beseech blessed Mary ever Virgin, blessed Michael the archangel, blessed John the Baptist, the holy apostles Peter and Paul, and all the saints, to pray for me to the Lord our God. Amen.]

CUT TO: INT. LADY CHAPEL, WHITEHALL PALACE – NIGHT

ELIZABETH prays and listens to the music.

CUT TO: INT. CORRIDOR, WHITEHALL PALACE – NIGHT

We see one of NORFOLK's MEN standing by a pillar. Suddenly the shadow of one of WALSINGHAM's MEN appears; NORFOLK's MAN falls to the ground as he is stabbed from behind.

INT. LAVATORIES – NIGHT

WALSINGHAM's MEN walk in … SUSSEX is still at his stool, his hose round his ankles. As he tries to grab his sword, they press their swords to his chest and throat.

SUSSEX looks at them. Then he suddenly screams in frustration.

CUT TO: INT. NORFOLK'S BEDCHAMBER, WHITEHALL PALACE – NIGHT

Through the drapes we again see NORFOLK and LETTICE in bed.

CUT TO: INT. GARDINER'S CELL, MONASTIC BUILDING – NIGHT

WALSINGHAM'S MEN enter quietly, to see the flayed, bloody back of BISHOP GARDINER. He turns towards them, and with a single thrust one of them runs him through with his sword. GARDINER falls against the wall. Dead.

CUT TO: CHOIRBOYS SINGING – MONTAGE SHOT

CUT TO: INT. ARUNDEL'S HOUSE – NIGHT

ARUNDEL and his wife lean over their sleeping CHILDREN. ARUNDEL's WIFE kisses them each gently on the forehead, without waking them. They leave the bedroom distraught, followed by a GUARD.

CUT TO: INT. NORFOLK'S BEDCHAMBER, WHITEHALL PALACE – NIGHT

NORFOLK and LETTICE are in bed, still making love. We pan up LETTICE's body as NORFOLK rolls over and LETTICE lies on top of him.

INT. CHAPEL, WHITEHALL PALACE – NIGHT

Close on ELIZABETH, tears streaking her face as the William Byrd mass soars to a climax. She rises, and departs.

INT. NORFOLK'S BEDCHAMBER, WHITEHALL PALACE – NIGHT

WALSINGHAM's MEN burst into the bedchamber, some with swords drawn. NORFOLK is in bed, with LETTICE beside him. LETTICE screams out and tries to cover herself. NORFOLK climbs out of bed and stares at them.

NORFOLK: What is the meaning of this?

WALSINGHAM appears.

WALSINGHAM: Your Grace is arrested. You must go with these men … to the Tower.

NORFOLK: I must do nothing, by your orders. I am Norfolk.

WALSINGHAM: You were Norfolk. Dead men have no titles.
(A beat) You are a traitor!

NORFOLK: Treason is an unforgiving thing, Walsingham! You had better have some proof of it.

Slowly, WALSINGHAM holds up the Pope's letter. NORFOLK glances at it, then looks over at LETTICE.

LETTICE lowers her eyes from his gaze and moves from the bed. WALSINGHAM's MEN take hold of NORFOLK.

WALSINGHAM: You were the most powerful man in England – and could have been greater still ... but you had not the courage to be loyal. Only the conviction of your own vanity.

NORFOLK: I think, Walsingham, a man's courage is in the manner of his death. I am content to die for my beliefs.
(A beat) So cut off my head and make me a martyr. The people will always remember it.

He stares at WALSINGHAM.
WALSINGHAM *(quietly)*: No. They will forget.

NORFOLK is led away. WALSINGHAM looks at LETTICE, then leaves.

CUT TO: INT. CELLARS – NIGHT

DUDLEY is drunk. He hears a door creak, and footsteps. He looks and sees WALSINGHAM.

DUDLEY: What kept you, Walsingham? I have been waiting ...

WALSINGHAM smiles. Then DUDLEY notices ELIZABETH. He gets up, has to steady himself against the edge of the table, and bows.

DUDLEY: Your Majesty ...

ELIZABETH: They are all gone to the Tower ... your friends. Tell me: how should I serve thee, Robert?

DUDLEY: My course is run.

ELIZABETH looks at him, in his drunkenness.

ELIZABETH: Just tell me: why?

DUDLEY: Why? ... Madam, is it not plain enough to you? ... It is no easy thing, to be loved by the Queen! It would corrupt the soul of any man, especially ... if he were vain, ambitious ... and weak.
  Now, for God's sake, kill me! There is nothing more now that life can show me, that is not already spoilt.

ELIZABETH (*after a beat*): No. I think rather to let you live.

WALSINGHAM: Madam, that is not wise. He must be made example of.

ELIZABETH: And I will … make an example of him! He shall be kept alive to always remind me of how close I came to danger.

A beat. She turns away and goes up the stairs. She walks past WALSINGHAM on the balcony and he turns and exits after her.

CUT TO: INT. CELL, TOWER OF LONDON – DAY

ARUNDEL comforts his WIFE. A PRIEST stands near them. The door is unlocked and opens. ELIZABETH enters. ARUNDEL crosses the room and kneels before her. His WIFE follows.

ARUNDEL: Your Majesty knows that I did it only for my faith, nothing more.

ELIZABETH holds out her hand. ARUNDEL kisses her ring.

ELIZABETH: All your many kindnesses to me are remembered.

ELIZABETH moves to ARUNDEL's WIFE, who is crying, and puts a comforting hand on her head.

ELIZABETH (*cont'd*)**:** You must not think we care not for your children.

His WIFE smiles through her tears.

LADY ARUNDEL: Your Majesty is merciful and forgiving.

ELIZABETH goes to the door. She gives a look to ARUNDEL. We see ARUNDEL, a flicker of hope in his eyes. The room dims to blackness as she goes out.

CUT TO: EXT. TOWER OF LONDON – DAY

NORFOLK lays his head upon the block. We see a flash of steel – his eyes still piercing – and it is over.

Cut to: the camera panning, showing the heads of the traitors, among them NORFOLK and SUSSEX.

Finally the camera rests on one head that wears a saintly expression. It is ARUNDEL.

INT. LADY CHAPEL, WHITEHALL PALACE – DAY

ELIZABETH sits alone, a solitary figure framed by pools of light, a statue of the Virgin Mary standing beside the altar. WALSINGHAM enters; she perceives his presence … but does not move.

ELIZABETH: How do I save myself? Am I to be made of stone, am I to be touched by nothing?

WALSINGHAM: All men need something greater than themselves to look up to and worship.

WALSINGHAM moves close to her.

WALSINGHAM *(cont'd)*: They must be able to touch the divine, here on earth, or they are like men of straw, blown this way and that …

ELIZABETH: She had such power over men's hearts. They died for her. Is this love to be hidden?
A beat. WALSINGHAM looks at her calmly.

WALSINGHAM: They have found nothing to replace her.

WALSINGHAM makes a move towards ELIZABETH. She does not respond. He leaves. ELIZABETH sits alone in silence.

CUT TO: INT. ELIZABETH'S BEDCHAMBER, WHITEHALL PALACE – NIGHT

Close on ELIZABETH, sitting before a mirror, wearing only a simple white shift. She stares at herself – as if seeing herself for the last time. ELIZABETH's face is expressionless, but KAT is tremulous.

KAT: Lady Mortimer has been sent to the Tower.

ELIZABETH looks at her.

KAT: She is with child.

ELIZABETH's expression does not change.

ELIZABETH: I will have none about me who are not chaste.

KAT begins to cry, then starts to cut off Elizabeth's hair, in long strands. A long beat.

ELIZABETH: Do not cry, sweet Kat. Do not be afraid. Come now. Sssh. Kat, do not cry. Leave me! Kat!

KAT starts to leave. Suddenly ELIZABETH holds out her hand to KAT and KAT grasps it. Close on KAT as she kisses her hands … .and then, very slowly, lets go.
  Close on ELIZABETH staring at her reflection in the mirror. Her head is bald. KAT is watching from a distance.

ELIZABETH: Look. I am become a virgin.

INT. GREAT HALL, WHITEHALL PALACE – DAY

The court is packed with people – silent, expectant. And then a gasp goes up – a great exhalation of surprise and powerful amazement. We see on the COURTIERS' faces looks of awe …
  And now, as she slowly moves forward, we see ELIZABETH. She has been transformed into the icon we know from history. Utterly changed.
  The white dress with its stiff high ruff, encrusted with pearls the size of pears. The red wig. The face so stiff and white with lead paste that it has become a mask, like porcelain. Pearls in her hair, swathes of pearls around her neck. Jewels gleaming on her dress and fingers.
  We see the reaction. The COURTIERS fall to their knees in genuine and not merely formal obeisance, as if before a goddess. ELIZABETH drifts forward, the guarantee and personification of her power. She sees CECIL, on his knees. She pauses, offers her hand.

ELIZABETH: Observe, my good Lord Burghley. I am married … to England.

CECIL, deeply moved, kisses her hand.

CECIL: Most gracious Sovereign Lady.

She moves on, passing DUDLEY, who is also on his knees before her, glancing as she passes.

ELIZABETH: Lord Robert …

DUDLEY: My lady.

Kat Ashley (Emily Mortimer)

She continues on her journey to the throne – passing WALSINGHAM. She stops when she reaches the throne and turns to the court.

ELIZABETH: My Lords – these two years God has both prospered and protected you with good success, under our direction. And we nothing doubt that the same maintaining hand will guide you still – and bring you to the ripeness of perfection.

ELIZABETH sits upon the throne – while the whole court still remain on their knees before her. She looks at them. We freeze on the mask.
    These words appear on the screen:

ELIZABETH REIGNED FOR ANOTHER FORTY YEARS. BY THE TIME OF HER DEATH, ENGLAND WAS THE RICHEST, MOST POWERFUL COUNTRY IN EUROPE.

SHE NEVER MARRIED. HER REIGN HAS BEEN CALLED "THE GOLDEN AGE."

SHE OUTLIVED BOTH WALSINGHAM AND DUDLEY.

WALSINGHAM REMAINED HER MOST TRUSTED AND LOYAL ADVISER UNTIL HIS DEATH.

ELIZABETH NEVER SAW DUDLEY AGAIN IN PRIVATE, BUT ON HER DEATHBED SHE BREATHED HIS NAME.

THE END

CAST AND CREW LIST

Principal Cast (In Order Of Appearance)

Bishop Gardiner	Terence Rigby
Duke of Norfolk	Christopher Eccleston
Lettice Howard	Amanda Ryan
Queen Mary of Tudor	Kathy Burke
Alvaro de la Quadra	James Frain
Earl of Sussex	Jamie Foreman
Earl of Arundel	Edward Hardwicke
Robert Dudley, Earl of Leicester	Joseph Fiennes
Isabel Knollys	Kelly Macdonald
Dance Tutor	Wayne Sleep
Elizabeth I	Cate Blanchett
Kat Ashley	Emily Mortimer
Sir Francis Walsingham	Geoffrey Rush
Sir William Cecil	Richard Attenborough
Waad, Chancellor of the Exchequer	Angus Deayton
Monsieur De Foix	Eric Cantona
Sir Thomas Elyot	Kenny Doughty
Mary of Guise	Fanny Ardant
Duc D'Anjou	Vincent Cassel
The Pope	John Gielgud
John Ballard	Daniel Craig

Other Cast (In Order Of Appearance)

Female Martyr	Liz Giles
Master Ridley	Rod Culbertson
Male Martyr	Paul Fox
Palace Chamberlain	Peter Stockbridge
King Philip II of Spain	George Yiasoumi
Mary's Dwarf	Valerie Gale
Lady In Waiting	Sally Grey
Lady In Waiting	Kate Loustau
Lady In Waiting	Elika Gibbs
Lady In Waiting	Sarah Owen
Lady In Waiting	Lily Allen
Master Of The Tower	Joe White
Norfolk's Man	Matt Andrews
Norfolk's Man	Liam Foley
Young French Man	Ben Frain
Priest	Lewis Jones
Bishop Carlisle	Michael Beint
Elizabeth's Dwarf	Hayley Burroughs
Earl Of Derby	Joseph O'Connor
Lord William Howard	Brendan O'Hea
Lord Harewood	Edward Highmore
First Bishop	Daniel Moynihan
Second Bishop	Jeremy Hawk
Bishop (In Cellar)	James Rowe
Third Bishop	Donald Pelmear
Handsome Man	Tim Bevan
Dudley's Man	Charles Cartmell
Dudley's Man	Edward Purver
Vatican Cardinal	Vladimir Vega
Arundel's Son	Alfie Allen
Arundel's Daughter	Daisy Bevan
Arundel's Nursemaid	Jennifer Lewicki
Arundel's Wife	Viviane Horne
Walsingham's Man	Nick Smallman

Crew

Director	Shekhar Kapur
Producers	Alison Owen
	Eric Fellner
	Tim Bevan
Written by	Michael Hirst
Director Of Photography	Remi Adefarasin Bsc
Production Designer	John Myhre
Editor	Jill Bilcock
Costume Designer	Alexandra Byrne
Music by	David Hirschfelder
Casting by	Vanessa Pereira
	Simone Ireland
Line Producer	Mary Richards
Co Producers	Debra Hayward
	Liza Chasin
First Assistant Director	Tommy Gormley
Sound Recordist	David Stephenson
Camera Operator	Philip Sindall
Location Manager	Sue Quinn
Financial Controller	Maggie Phelan
Make Up & Hair Designer	Jenny Shircore
Associate Editor	Justin Krish
Casting France	Kate Dowd
Post Production Supervisor	Michael Solinger
Choreography	Sue Lefton
Executive In Charge Of Production	Jane Frazer
Focus Puller	Julian Bucknall
Clapper Loader	James Bloom
Key Grip	John Arnold
Camera Trainee	John Adefarasin
2nd Camera Operator	Sean Savage
2nd Focus Puller	Ben Wilson
2nd Clapper Loaders	Iain Struthers
	Oliver Loncraine
	Ron Fleet
2nd Grip	Andy Young
Script Supervisor	Pat Rambaut
Continuity Assistant	Zoe Morgan
2nd Unit Continuity Trainee	Kate Dimmock
Boom Operator	Gerry Bates
Sound Assistant	Thomas Gastinel
2nd Unit Sound Recording	Tommy Staples
	Mike Harris
	Dick Hunt
Production Co-Ordinator	Simon Fraser
Production Assistants	Karen McLuskey
	Tracey Tucker
Alison Owen's Assistant	Jennifer Lewicki
Mr. Bevan's Assistant	Juliette Dow
Mr. Fellner's Assistant	Lara Thompson
Mr. Kapur's Assistant	Liam Foley
Production Runner	Ben Ogley
Re-Shoot Production Managers	Erica Bensly
	Laura Julian
Post Production Coordinator	Jatinderpal Chohan
2nd Unit Director	Ian Madden
2nd Assistant Director	Mark Layton
2nd Assistant Director/ Crowd Casting	Sue Wood
3rd Assistant Director	Sarah Purser
3rd Assistant Director	Harry Boyd
Floor Runner	Alex Oakley
Crowd Casting Assistant Director	Lisa Jones
Crowd Runner	Lisa Tolin
2nd Unit Assistant Director	David Gilchrist
Company Coordinator	Nina Khoshaba
Senior Vice President Of Business Affairs	Angela Morrison
Vice President Of Business Affairs	Rachel Holroyd
Directors Of Finance	Rashid Chinchanwala
	Julian Tomlin
Production Accountant	Susan Nicholson
Assistant Accountants	Stephen Naulls
	Frances Richardson
	Jayne Barton
	Sarah Fleet
Post Production Accounts	Tarn Harper
Unit Managers	Michael Harm
	Christian McWilliams
Location Assistant	Joseph Jayawardena
Location Department Trainee	Simon August
Casting Assistant	Kate Bulpitt
Assistant To Mr. Rush	Jami Wrenn
First Assistant Editor	Kate Buckland
Second Assistant Editor	Celia Haining
Second Assistant Editor	Lionel Johnston
Cutting Room Trainee	Christopher Womack
Supervising Sound Editor	Mark Auguste

ADR Sound Editors	Tim Hands
	Derek Triggs
Assistant Sound Editors	Howard Halsall
	Sam Auguste
Music Consultant	Roger White
Music Editor	Mike Higham
Re-Recording Mixers	Mike Dawson
Voice Casting	Brendan Donnison
Post Production Consultant	Steve Harrow
Hair/Makeup Artists	Ivana Primorac
	Chrissie Whitney
	Lisa Pickering
	Christine Greenwood
	Karen Ferguson
	Miranda Davidson
	Anita Burger
Costume Design Director	Frank Gardiner
Assistant Costume Designer	Debbie Scott
Costume Buyer	Kay Manasseh
Wardrobe Supervisor	Suzi Turnbull
Wardrobe Mistress	Jane Petrie
Wardrobe Assistants	John Denison
	Katrina Frith
	Dan Grace
	Hilary Guthrie
	Nick Heather
	Natalie Ward
	Berenice Wright
Head Pre-Fitter	Tim Aslam
Pre-Fitter	Rebecca Townsend
Costume Cutter	Annie Hadley
Costume Makers	Clare Banet, Sue Bradbear, Melanie Carter, Ruth Caswell, Lee Clayton, Gill Crawford, Gordon Garforth, Jane Grimshaw, Andrew Joslin, Penelope King, Linda Lashley, Tibor Mate, Sue Meyer, Tanya Mould, Anne Nichols, Marcia Smith, Roslyn Tidy, Suzanna Wilson, Dominic Young & Cosprops Limited
Costume Runners	Dora Schweitzer
	Suki Gardiner
Dyeing	Gabrielle Firth
	Mathilde Sandberg
Millinery	Sean Barrett
Jewellery Made by	Ericson Beamon & Martin Adams

Supervising Art Director	Jonathan Lee
Art Director	Lucy Richardson
Assistant Art Directors	Poppy Luard
	Sarah Hauldren
Storyboard Artist	Temple Clark
Draughtsmen	Mike Stallion
	Matt Gray
Junior Draughtsman	Stuart Kearns
Art Department Co-ordinator	Nicola Barnes
Art Department Assistant	Shana Nieberg
Set Decorator	Peter Howitt
Production Buyers	Belinda Edwards
	Peter Ruherford
Property Master	David Balfour
Props Storeman	Keith Vowles
Supervising Dressing Propman	John Wells
Dressing Propmen	John Knight
	Laurence Wells
	Kevin Wheeler
	Marlon Cole
Props Trainee	Gregor Telfer
Drapes Master	Anthony Szuch
Food Stylist	Debbie Brodie
Standby Propmen	Barry Arnold
	Colin Burgess
Construction Manager	Andy Evans
Assistant Construction Manager	Ian Green
Construction Buyer	Rob Allen
Supervising Carpenters	Gary Pledger
	David Edwards
Chargehand Carpenter	Anthony Mansey
Carpenters	John Addison, Joe Alley, Daryl Carter, Chris Corke, Martin Day, John Franklin, Michael Gooch, Gavin Gordon, Fred Gunning, Ralph Harrison, Christopher Mansey, Andrew Mash, Alfred Pulis, Jeff Reid, Lee Reilly, Bernard Ryan, Barry Smalls, Dean Smith, Tony Snook, Robert Wright
Apprentice Carpenter	Mark Green
Supervising Painters	Paul Wiltshire
	John Campbell

Painters	Stuart Blinco, Adam Campbell, Glyn Evans, Giovanni Giaccotto, Anthony Goddard, Lee Goddard, Graham Pearce, Cornelius Restall, John Shergold, Steven Sibley, Clive Whitbread
Painters' Labourer	Harry Alley
Supervising Riggers	Jose A Romera Abuin, Kevin Welch
Riggers	Mark Buchan, Martin Goddard, Ron Miles, John Pitt, David Price, Ken Serth, Reg Smith, Andrew Weller
Supervising Stagehand	Colin Smith
Chargehand Stagehand	Raymond Branch
Stagehands	Michael Bailey, Steve Bovingdon, Ricky Dunning, Clifford Rashbrook, Larry Rashbrook, Danny Smith, Roy Smith
Standby Carpenter	John Casey
Standby Painter	Brian Groves
Standby Riggers	David Weller, Peter Grafham
Standby Stagehand	Brian Webb
Sculptors	Fred Evans, Roy Rodgers
Assistant Sculptor	Tracy Ann Baines
Supervising Plasterer	Kenny Powell
Chargehand Plasterer	Bill Bush
Plasterers	Stan Apperley, John Harris, Derek O'Reilly, Jamie Powell, Steve Powell, Bob Rose, Colin Smith, Andy Tombs
Plasterers' Labourers	John Brown, Bill Thompson
Scenic Artist	Brian Bishop
Gaffer Electrician	Jimmy Wilson
Best Boy	Mitch Spooner
Electricians	Ian Franklin, Bob Hunt, Martin Welland, Pat Deveney
Generator Operators	Mark Hutton, Ron Savory
Rigging Gaffer Electrician	Barrie More
Rigging Electricians	Billy Thornhill, Chris Allkins, Steve Senior
Electrical Rigger	Bob Debelius
Senior SFX Technicians	David Watson, Steve Paton, Peter Skehan
Junior SFX Technician	David Watson Jr.
SFX Trainees	John Keating, Richard Stanbury
Dialogue Coach	Penny Dyer
Assistant Choreographer	Diana Scrivener
Researcher	Justin D. Pollard
Tutor/Chaperone	Samantha Rushton
Unit Publicist	Patric Scott
Stills Photographer	Alex Bailey
Health & Safety Officer	Cyril Gibbons
Health & Safety Advisors	Paul Jackson, Yazdi Nash, Jake Edmonds
Unit Nurses	Suzanna Freeborn, Jordan Archer
Stand-Ins	Viviane Horne, Steve Morphew, Joe Lacey, Dean Taylor
Stunt Co-ordinator	Terry Forrestal
Stunt Performers (in alphabetical order)	Andy Bennet, Richard Bradshaw, Steve Caswell, Simon Crane, Gabriel Cronnelly, Danielle Da Costa, Ray De Haan, Neil Finnegan, Steve Griffin, Nick Hobbs, Sy Hollands, Rowley Irlam, Vincent Keane, Derek Lea, Tom Lucy, Jo Mclaren, Peter Miles, Dominic Preece, Kieron Shah, C.C. Smiff, Rocky Taylor, Peter White, Will Willoughby
Special Effects Supervisor	George Gibbs
Visual Effects Supervisor	Peter Chiang
Visual Effects Cameraman	Stefan Lange
Digital Visual Effects by	Men In White Coats
Digital Visual Effects Compositors	Phil Attfield, Tom Hocking, Robin Beard, James Jordon

Digital Visual Effects Scanning/Recording	Gruff Owen
	Adam Christopher
Digital Visual Effects Producers	Steve Shaw
	Adrian Martin
Digital Visual Effects Co-ordinator	Rebecca Elliot
MIWC Finance Director	Lasairfhiona Lawless
3D Animation	Complete 3D
Animation Supervisor	Christopher Holmes
Animators	Steve Anderson
	Steve Street
	Brett Miller
Programmer	Pete Medrow
End Titles And Opticals by	General Screen Enterprises Film And Digital Effects Studios
Main Titles by	Passion Pictures
Transport Co-ordinators	Graham Fordham
	Dave Machin
Unit Drivers	Mike Beavan, Enyo Mortty, Terry Reece, John Smith, Peter Mercer
Facility Truck Drivers	Roger Hardman, Tony Moorhead, Bob Turner, Kelvin Cook, Bob Dean, Richard Titcombe, Ron Green, Mark West, John Cornelius, Mark Russell, Peter Adams, Mike Harris, Albert Smith, Scott Henley, Duncan Prentice, Andy Carter, Barry Stone, Chas Hughes, Frank Hughes, John Dawson, Paul Jones
Catering Supplied by	Set Meals
Catering Manager	Olivia Timberlake
Chef	Rebecca Wiseman
Catering Assistants	Marie Glen
	Kate Dimmock
Cameras And Lenses by	Arri-Media Limited
Originated On Motion Picture Film Supplied From	Kodak
Editing Equipment	Edit-Hire
Electrical Equipment	Lee Lighting Limited
Colour by	Technicolour Film Services
Negative Cutting	Sylvia Wheeler Negative Cutting Services
Colour Grader	Peter Hunt

Recorded At	Shepperton Sound Studios
Editing Facilities	De Lane Lea Limited
Stills Processing	Pinewood Stills
Transport/Facilities Supplied by	Lays International Ltd, Location Facilities Ltd, On-Set Location Services Ltd, Cavalier Transport, Focus Transport, Studio Workshops
Horses/Carriages Supplied by	Steve Dent
Animals Supplied by	Animals Okay
Boats Supplied by	Turk Film Services
Boats Masters	John Tweedle
	John Turk
Prosthetic Heads by	Animated Extras
Wig Makers	Terry Jarvis
	Sarah Phillips & Co
Contact Lenses	Clive Kay Opticians
Costumiers	Cosprops Limited, Angels & Bermans Limited, Costumi D'Arte – Rome, Cornejo, Nicolao Atelier – Venice, E. Rancati Srl, Sartoria Russo, Tirrelli Costumi Roma, Royal National Theatre, Royal Shakespeare Theatre
Shoes Supplied by	Pompei
Insurance Services Supplied by	Near North Entertainment
Legal Services Supplied by	Marriott Harrison – Rushes
Courier Services	Dynamic International
Made on location in	Northumberland, County Durham, Derbyshire, London and at Shepperton Studios, Shepperton, London, England
Assistant Music Director	Sam Schwarz
Orchestrations	David Hirschfelder
	Ric Formosa
Conductors	David Hirschfelder
	Ric Formosa
	Sam Schwarz
Music Copyists	John Thorn
	Gavin Cornish
Orchestra Leader	Nigel Mclean

Choirs	David Hobson Chorale
	Australian Boys Choir
Choir Master	John Dingle
Featured Soprano	Kim Wheeler
Featured Tenor	David Hobson
Sound Engineer	Robin Gray
	Chris Scallan
Music recorded at	Alan Eaton Studios,
	Melbourne, Australia

Executive In Charge Of
Music For Polygram
Filmed Entertainment   Dawn Sol

'Te Deum'
Written by Tallis
Performed by St. John's College Choir
Produced by Andrew Raburn
Published by Oxford University Press
Licensed Courtesy Of Decca Classics

'Domine Secundum Actum Meum'
Written by William Byrd
Produced by David Hirschfelder
Published by Polygram

'Requiem'
Written by Amadeus Mozart
Produced by David Hirschfelder
Published by Polygram

Original Soundtrack Available On Decca Records

Special Thanks to:
The Duke Of Northumberland, Alnwick Castle, Haddon
Hall, The Lady Armstrong, Bamburgh Castle, Northern
Region Of English Heritage And Aydon And Warkworth
Castle, Raby Castle, The Dean And Chapter Of Durham
Cathedral, Sir Humphry Wakefield Bt. And Chillingham
Castle, The Dean And Chapter Of York Minster,
The Landmark Arts Centre, Lavish Locations, Bolton
Castle, Dorney Court, Choristers From St. Peter's And
St. Olave's School York

Henry VIII by Hans Holbein the Younger supplied by
The Bridgeman Art Library
Spanish Armada used by permission of
The Worshipful Society of Apothecaries of London
A selection of Portraits by courtesy of
National Portrait Gallery, London

Credits not contractual.